To   of
drugs, we are experiencing an epidemic in
drug addiction among both teenagers and
young adults. The current war on drugs is at
once societal, communal, familial, and
individual.

Certainly the problem must be approached on
an individual basis, but unless we all work
together, the drug problem among today's
adolescent population will only intensify. We
owe young people a great deal more than that.
                              —*From the Preface*

TEEN ADDICTION

Marti Heuer

With a Foreword by Suzanne Somers

Formerly Titled: *Happy Daze*

BALLANTINE BOOKS • NEW YORK

To Ger, my love and my best friend.

The use of the male pronoun throughout the book is *not* meant to signify predominant male focus but rather is used to offer consistent reading.

Copyright © 1994 by Marti Heuer-Myers

All rights reserved under International and Pan-American Copyright Conventions. Published in the United States of America by Ballantine Books, a division of Random House, Inc., New York, and distributed in Canada by Random House of Canada Limited, Toronto. Originally published in 1985 by M. A. C. under the title *Happy Daze.*

Library of Congress Catalog Card Number: 94-96324

ISBN 0-345-36282-9

Manufactured in the United States of America

First Ballantine Books Edition: January 1995

10 9 8 7 6 5 4 3 2

Contents

Acknowledgments   vii
Foreword   ix
Preface   xiii

CHAPTER 1   The Beginnings of Dependency   1
CHAPTER 2   The Progression of Dependency   24
CHAPTER 3   The Dependent Adolescent   48
CHAPTER 4   Children of Alcoholics with
               Dependency Problems   73
CHAPTER 5   Enabling the Adolescent   97
CHAPTER 6   Learning the Hard Way—The Adolescent
               in Recovery   114
CHAPTER 7   The Beginnings of Wellness: The Family
               in Recovery   144
CHAPTER 8   Resources   158
CHAPTER 9   Healthy Perspectives   171

ACKNOWLEDGMENTS

This book is a dream that has been realized through the love and support of many people, people who believed in this book and in me. I would like to acknowledge a special few who were directly involved in the writing of *Teen Addiction*.

George Stewart, for his "gentle" persuasion in motivating me to write this manuscript.

Peg Bernhard, for her love, support, and encouragement.

Joyce Penrod, for her patience and the many hours spent typing the manuscript.

Claudia Black, for her direct feedback and for helping me to keep a "healthy perspective."

Jack Fahey, for his reading and rereadings, his guidance, feedback, and his enthusiasm.

Sharon Wegscheider-Cruse, for her "roles in the alcoholic family."

Gerry Myers, for his direction, creativeness, feedback, and for his ongoing love and support.

And last, I would like to acknowledge those young people whom I have laughed with, cried with, and cared about as they begin their process of recovery. They have made this dream a reality.

Foreword

Since the release of my book, *Keeping Secrets*, in 1988, I have traveled throughout the country to speak about my early years growing up in an alcoholic family. My audiences have included adults who also grew up in families where there was alcoholism and, often, emotional, physical, or sexual abuse. Their strong commitment to create healthier families than the ones in which they grew up is obvious from their questions.

Yet these adults and many others continue to struggle with the age-old question, "Why do kids use alcohol and drugs?" The issue seems to be especially difficult for parents who experienced the trauma of parental alcoholism as children. They cannot grasp why their own children would begin using alcohol and drugs, especially when they know the family history and the consequences.

Despite their parents' personal experiences, many young people decide to use alcohol and drugs. The information offered in *Teen Addiction* will help parents identify what a son's or daughter's addiction may look like, since many parents admit that, regrettably, they are often the last ones to know that their children are in serious trouble. Parental denial still runs deep.

In this straightforward book, Marti Heuer presents information that is practical and, at the same time, disarming. We begin to see young people as individuals with feelings and emotions that they cover up with alcohol and other drugs. We also begin to understand that their negative behavior is usually dictated by their addiction.

Teen Addiction provides us with a nonjudgmental, yet truthful look at these problems while offering solutions and resources. Any parent, peer, teacher, counselor, law enforcement officer, physician, or mental-health worker will benefit from the knowledge that this book imparts.

Marti provides us with a thorough knowledge of the problem by sharing her many years of experience of working with young people in schools, juvenile court systems, and alcohol- and drug-treatment programs. Her knowledge allows for a broader definition of understanding concerning adolescents who experience alcohol and drug problems.

Through my own personal experiences with alcoholism in our family, it has become increasingly clear to me that we can no longer point our finger at parents, schools, or our children's friends as "the problem." The problem of adolescent addiction confronts educators, social workers, families, and juvenile justice personnel. Teenage alcohol and drug use does not just impact individual families. It affects entire communities. And remember: no one is immune from potentially developing an addiction to alcohol and other drugs, regardless of age.

Some youth are just beginning to use drugs or are experimenting with crack, cocaine, methamphetamines, or heroin. Some are "just using alcohol" and do not believe they will suffer consequences, often despite their family histories of alcoholism. Many youths are still suffering and have not yet found their way to freedom.

We all must respond to the epidemic of youth alcohol and drug use, and along with it, the increase in youth violence, crime, and gang involvement. We begin to understand that we are all responsible for the future of our young people by helping to make them responsible for their own actions and behavior.

Throughout the book, Marti helps us realize that each of us can play a part in the solution by understanding why today's youth become abusers. We can take the next step by learning how to respond to this problem. Once we as individuals understand the dynamics of adolescent addiction, we can begin to assume a collective approach to solving the problem and take steps toward implementing lasting successes with our young people.

Teen Addiction will be of great value to parents and families. It will provide valuable insights for anyone raising children today or anyone who is considering raising a family in the future. Even though your child may not have a problem with alcohol or drugs, the information and insight offered throughout *Teen Addiction* will help you do a better job of parenting. If I'd had this book to read years ago when I was raising my son, I would certainly have had a better understanding of how to respond to him during his teenage years.

Marti offers knowledge and hope as she describes not only the problem but the solutions and resources that are available to anyone concerned about a teenager's potential addiction to alcohol or other drugs. This book will become a resource for anyone involved with young people.

SUZANNE SOMERS

Preface

The field of chemical dependency has passed through several transitions in the past twenty years, ranging from the identification and acceptance of alcohol as a drug in the 1950s, to the emergence in the 1960s and 1970s of more "sophisticated" drugs such as LSD and marijuana, to the current "crack" epidemic of the 1980s and 1990s.

Professional treatment and prevention approaches have likewise progressed through a series of changes since the 1950s, from the initial Twelve Step–based groups to the therapeutic communities and outpatient settings of the 1970s to the acute-care chemical dependency treatment programs of the 1980s. All of these treatment programs focused primarily on providing adult services and often ignored the needs of teenagers and young adults, who were perceived to be simply "experimenting" with mood- and mind-altering drugs. "Kids will be kids," was the prevailing philosophy of the time.

With the acceptance in the early 1980s of alcohol as a drug responsible for a chemical dependency, adolescent chemical dependency was identified as a disease unto itself. Parents and entire communities began to mobilize against adolescent drug use, and today community services geared specifically to the adolescent population are available in the majority of states throughout the country.

Now the entire nation is involved in the "war on drugs."

The family as a unit has become critical to the identification and treatment of chemical dependency problems. Addiction has been identified as a family disease, its influence and impact all too often manifested in child abuse, domestic violence, and, most important, the generational cycle of alcoholism and other chemical dependencies. Parents and human-services providers have at last validated the disease of chemical dependency in adolescents, affording it the same professional attention they would any other medical disease.

Today, with the availability and minimal cost of drugs such as cocaine and crack, we are experiencing an epidemic in drug addictions among both teenagers and young adults. Gangs, once thought of solely in relation to the turbulent 1950s and 1960s, are now prevalent in small and large cities alike, and their role in drug trafficking merely compounds the dilemma facing us.

The current war on drugs is at once societal, communal, familial, and individual. Certainly addiction must be approached on an individual basis, but unless we all work together, the drug problem among today's adolescent population will only intensify. We owe young people a great deal more than that.

CHAPTER 1

The Beginning of Dependency

"I didn't know then what I know now. In some ways, I wasn't ready for all of this. Sobriety means life to me. What I was doing before wasn't living ... at least not like I'm living today. I used to take a drink or smoke a joint whenever things weren't going my way, which was most of the time, back then.

I've been sober for fourteen months now. I can honestly say that things are getting better for me. Some days are better than others, but I don't want to go back to living like that ever again. I'm still scared, and the people in my AA group say that my fear is healthy because I should never forget where I came from. When I was first sober, I couldn't imagine not using for even one day. I was scared and angry. I kept thinking, Why me? but, day by day, both good and bad, I faced life without chemicals and alcohol. I started to get well.

Today, I have more happy days and fewer sad days. When I do have sad or hard days, I am still grateful for my sobriety, because I worked so hard to get to this point. I'm happy with my new life, but most of all, I'm happy with me."

Craig—age 18

Addiction to a chemical—whether it be alcohol, cocaine, marijuana, or amphetamines—is characterized by

an inability to control the usage despite harmful consequences. In the chemical dependency treatment profession, an addiction to alcohol and other chemicals is
defined as a disease in that it is primarily progressive in
nature and if left untreated can be fatal. In 1956 the
American Medical Association proclaimed alcoholism
and other drug addictions as diseases. Since that time,
acceptance from the general public has been slow. Alcoholics and drug addicts are still perceived stereotypi-
cally, as skid row bums or heroin junkies. In point of
fact less than 5 percent of the alcoholic or drug-
dependent population fits this category. Moreover, alcoholism and drug dependencies are not restricted by age,
race, social status, or gender. Addictions can be found
in any family situation or any family member, regardless of age. Adolescents possess the same capabilities to
develop addictions to alcohol and other chemicals as do
their adult counterparts. Unfortunately this aspect of the
disease is still misunderstood.

*Peter, fifteen years old, seemed to be the least likely
candidate for alcohol and drug addictions. He was a
football player at his high school and had played on the
team for three years. As a senior, he missed football
practices and had little interest in the game. Peter pre-
ferred cocaine to any drug that he had tried. He used
cocaine and alcohol as often as he could, subsidizing
his habit through wages from his part-time job and even
stealing money from his parents to buy his chemicals.*

*Peter did not want to stop using chemicals and was
ultimately referred to an inpatient treatment setting for
drug-dependent youths. His father, a recovering alcoholic for three years, insisted that Peter go into treatment or find a place to live other than their home.*

Peter was cross-addicted to cocaine and alcohol. He

did not think he had a problem. He had been using for only a year and a half. His father was an alcoholic, but Peter rationalized that he was too young to have a serious problem with alcohol and drugs. He believed that he could stop using the alcohol and cocaine if he really wanted to. He just wasn't ready to quit yet. "Besides," Peter stated, "I don't use nearly as much as some of my friends."

Peter—age 15

Peter is not unique. Most adolescents enter treatment in denial of their disease, honestly believing that they are different and can learn to control their chemical usage.

The X-factor theory of chemical dependency incorporates a number of possible reasons for dependency, including genetic predisposition, psychological learning to relieve pain and emotional trauma, and chemical vulnerability.

Genetic Predisposition

Genetic predisposition supposes a genetic basis for the addiction to alcohol and other mood-altering chemicals. Under this theory, a gene is present and is passed from one generation to another much like genes predisposing cancer, heart disease, and diabetes. This gene triggers the disease once alcohol and other drug usage begins.

The theory of genetic predisposition has gained credibility thanks to a recent report published in the *Journal of the American Medical Association*. Researchers found a link between the presence of a receptor gene for dopamine (a neurotransmitter in the brain associated with pleasure-seeking behaviors) and alcoholism. Of individuals with this gene, the report states, 77 percent were alcoholics; only 28 percent of those without the gene were alcoholics.[1]

Evidence of genetic influence in the disease of alcoholism was present fifteen to twenty years ago with studies such as one completed in Sweden of 1,775 adoptees. Findings showed that children born to alcoholic parents but adopted by nonalcoholics were at least six times more likely to develop the disease of alcoholism than were members of the general population. Similar studies completed in the United States have found that Children of Alcoholics have up to four times the risk of developing alcoholism and other chemical addictions than do children of nonalcoholic parents.[2]

This recent research clearly establishes alcoholism as a disease and adds increasing evidence that genetic factors are as important as environmental factors in predisposing people to the disease. These findings could lead to the development of a blood test to detect the presence of genes associated with alcoholism and other chemical dependencies. Tests such as these could provide children predisposed to alcoholism with tangible information that would assist them in making healthy decisions concerning the use of alcohol and other drugs.

It is important to note that there is no physical or psychological craving for the drug prior to the ingestion of mood-altering chemicals. Thus it is believed that abstinence from chemicals could prevent addictive developments for the adolescent. For some Children of Alcoholics, making the decision not to drink or use mood-altering chemicals may be the best choice, given the family's propensity for alcoholism and drug addiction.

Psychological Predisposition

This component of the X-factor theory suggests that addiction may, in some cases, be a learned behavior. Individuals searching for mechanisms to cope with perceived unmanageable issues may turn to alcohol and other drugs as a solution and may eventually incorporate this "problem-solving" technique into their lifestyle. Of course, such a coping mechanism results in both physical and psychological addiction to chemicals. In time the addiction itself becomes primary but remains unidentified in the face of problems dictating the chemical usage.

Risk factors for adolescents who will develop problems with alcohol and other chemicals increase when certain characteristics are present.[3] Some areas that may serve as additional stressors for young people include:

Family Management Problems. Families that provide unclear or inconsistent rules for expected behavior confuse the child. Although often bragged about to peers and friends, lax supervision or monitoring of activities may actually be perceived by the adolescent as indifference. Inconsistent reactions to behaviors that include excessive discipline and criticism may contribute to the adolescent's negative self-image and further preclude the child from developing positive actions and behavior as a response to stress.

Friends Who Use Drugs. Initial experimentation with drug(s) most frequently happens through the influence of close friends. Attitudes of acceptance are often communicated both verbally and nonverbally from friends as well as family members. Children who need to belong will find it difficult not to join in and will not want to risk rejection. Many adolescents are unprepared psychologically to face rejection from close peers in almost any situation.

Parental Drug Use. Parental modeling of drug and alcohol use, especially when a child is involved (the son who gets his father a beer from the refrigerator), increases the potential for that child to accept the use of alcohol and drugs later on. Moreover, positive parental attitudes toward the use of substances increases the child's comfort level with their use. Children of Alcoholics are particularly "set up" to perceive alcohol and other drug use as a means of solving frustrations and problems. In some cases, however, the child of an alcoholic parent will move to the other extreme and literally "not touch" alcohol or other drugs. A strong negative reaction does not, however, automatically limit the risk of developing an addiction. Such a child's contempt may actually move him closer psychologically to developing a relationship with the hated substances at some time in the future.

Academic Failure. Children who fail at school because of boredom, lack of ability, or lack of confidence in their abilities are at higher risk to develop a drug problem as a coping mechanism to an intolerable daily situation.

The use of drugs as a mechanism to deal with feelings of insecurity, feelings of failure, and internal conflict and confusion may result in both physical and psychological addictions to chemicals for high-risk youth. The strong psychological "setup" to use drugs can also be found in peer groups, where feeling accepted is paramount, in some cases even stronger than family bonds.

Other environmental factors may play a role in predisposing a young person to the use of chemicals as a life-style. Adolescents growing up in the face of gang violence will often not question the values of family, opting simply to continue the cycle of gang involvement and drug addiction. Associating with their gang allows them to experience the emotional bonding they are unable to find in their immediate families. It also "empowers" them in a way they cannot achieve through school or employment. The sense of power they are able to feel in bonding with other gang members may be just as addicting for some youths as the eventual downward spiral of chemical dependency.

Gangs exist throughout the country but are particularly visible in large urban areas. Many adolescents will seek respect by joining gangs and then experience the need to prove themselves by punishing someone outside the gang for an act of disrespect. It is this use of power that is destroying communities, innocent victims, families, and the gang members themselves. Adolescents growing up in such an environment stand little chance to escape the influence of gangs and drug involvement. Many of these high-risk youths are never given the opportunity to know another way of life.

Chemical Vulnerability

The third component of the X-factor theory focuses on the inability of certain individuals to tolerate physically even small amounts of a chemical, including alcohol. Persons with this susceptibility often experience exaggerated mood swings and personality changes while under the influence of chemicals. Thus a soft-spoken man may become loud and abrasive after one or two beers, and a shy, quiet woman may berate her husband verbally while under the influence of 20 milligrams of Demerol following surgery. Such individuals generally return to their original mood once they are sober and chemical free.

Persons with this component of the X-factor may also experience blackouts while under the influence of alcohol and drugs. The blackouts, periods in which the person cannot remember what he did, what he said, where he went, and whom he talked with, may occur occasionally or frequently and may last a short time, several minutes or less, or much longer. Blackouts are considered one of the earliest warning signs of the onset of the disease: persons who begin to experience blackouts with the ingestion of small amounts of alcohol and other chemicals are being given valuable information about how their metabolism is handling alcohol and drugs.

Certain ethnic groups may be especially vulnerable to the effects of chemicals. The Native American population has been both directly and indirectly affected by alcoholism for generations. According to statistics from the Native American National Association for Children of Alcoholics, over 50 percent of the Native American population is affected by the disease. The Native American's relationship and chemical vulnerability to alcohol has created generational problems associated with drinking that far surpass those in any other minority.[4]

Any one or combination of these three factors may result in the development of addiction to alcohol or other chemicals. Other theories exist in the annals of psychiatry and psychology that view addictions as symptoms of more severe personality disorders. Although this may be true in some cases, the majority of professionals in the chemical dependency treatment field have accepted the X-factor theory of chemical addiction, which in turn has helped alleviate the stigma associated with chemical dependency. Acceptance of the disease concept allows individuals to seek treatment more readily by removing many of the negative preconceptions associated with addictions.

Cultural Considerations

Treatment of alcoholism and drug dependencies in the adult population is much more widely accepted, as evidenced by the growing number of employee assistance programs in the work setting, as well as the number of specialized programs that treat minority populations. Specialized programming and increased sensitivity toward cultural considerations of minority populations is at last gaining ground in the treatment of adult alcoholic and drug dependent persons. Since many of these programs have been in existence for ten years or more, statistics exist to provide program administration with valuable information about minority populations' responses to treatment and their chances for achieving and maintaining sobriety.

Native Americans

Alcohol abuse is a leading cause of health problems among Native American populations. According to the National Center of Health statistics, four of the top ten causes of death among Native American people may be related directly to alcohol abuse: suicide, homicide, cirrhosis of the liver, and accidents. Alcoholism and other drug addictions are also responsible for violence, unemployment, arrests, and, ultimately, the devastation of an entire people. Many treatment specialists who work with the Native American population believe that a combination of community unity, American Indian spirituality, individual accountability, and Twelve Step groups are needed to offer an effective treatment approach.

The National Center for Health statistics show that among Native American women and youths, alcohol is still more serious. Women accounted for almost half the deaths from cirrhosis of the liver, compared to about one-third of cirrhosis deaths among African American and Caucasian women. In the Native American culture, women are expected to remain strong and stoic in the face of adversity: alcohol and drugs may give them permission to be angry, hurt, sad, even violent; the drugs may allow them to be "human." Thus, findings report that Native American women are more likely to die of cirrhosis at an earlier age than are black or white women, as they have rates of cirrhosis of the liver thirty-six times that of Caucasian females.

What is happening among Native American youths is even more pronounced. Some children begin chemical usage as early as age nine, using inhalants such as gases and glues, which may cause organic brain damage, and thus diminish the child's ability to remember, think, and reason. Many of these high-risk youths come from generations of relatives who were drug dependent and alcoholic; they are simply continuing the legacy. Intervention and prevention programs designed to reach the thousands of children growing up in alcoholic families must be implemented if we are to begin reversing the statistics of this proud minority population.

Hispanic Populations

Hispanics now compose approximately 8 percent of the population of the United States. The increase in chemical dependency within this culture is visible in all parts of the country. Although there is no such thing as a typical Hispanic, recurring patterns may be found when addressing this population, patterns that may provide treatment approaches that will best suit the needs of the Hispanic seeking help.

Seeking help may be especially difficult for a Hispanic male, whose culture attaches disgrace to anyone identified as an alcoholic. The female, who is accorded a less prestigious position in the culture, may also find it difficult to go beyond the family to seek help and will therefore rarely be found in treatment centers. Since the Hispanic population in general is less likely to seek professional therapy than other populations as a whole, additional efforts must be made to acknowledge that treatment may be threatening for them. Admitting defeat with an addiction may be seen as a moral weakness. Consequently the solution will most likely involve alternatives other than seeking professional help for a disease.

The level of denial of the disease of alcoholism may impede intervention with adults and most certainly with adolescent Hispanics who are heading down the self-destructive path toward chemical addiction. Programs that are culturally sensitive to the Hispanic are needed, as many presently must recover with assistance from their churches and other outside sources, rather than through a treatment program that addresses their needs.[6]

African Americans

Alcoholism is often believed to be the number-one health, mental health, and social problem among African Americans in this country. The destruction caused by crack and cocaine for adults and youth alike still does not compare to the damage done by alcohol in the African American community. Alcohol continues to destroy lives and entire families in greater proportion than any other drug within this population. This becomes more evident in looking at the other major issues affecting the community: an increase in violence and gangs, unemployment and poor health care, and high rates of child abuse and neglect.

Treatment programs that provide services to African American communities have a responsibility to become educated in the cultural and psychological aspects of addiction for them. The level of denial for both adults and adolescents must be addressed by treatment programs if they are to attain a chemically free life-style. According to James H. Evans, author of *Counseling the Black Client*, we need "more programs and agencies in the black community, more recovering black counselors as role models, and more aware and sensitive nonblack counselors." With such changes happening, albeit slowly, more African Americans can hope to achieve sobriety.

Those who address the needs of the community must understand that many African Americans enter treatment at a late stage in the disease of alcoholism and drug addiction. Adolescents entering treatment may also be seriously involved with gangs and be seeking treatment to "hide out" until things on the street cool down. Motivation for treatment must be explored with the adolescent, along with the need to incorporate a sense of self-worth and pride in one's heritage.[7]

Specialized programs for adolescents have become more prevalent, but often there are fewer resources to treat the disease. This seems to be particularly true for adolescents who are being raised in rural areas. Contrary to popular belief, there is a serious chemical abuse problem in the rural areas of most states, with relatively few treatment services designed to meet the needs of an adolescent population.

Even with an increased focus nationally on "Just Say No to Drugs" campaigns and other community awareness programs designed to educate children and parents on the effects of drug-taking behavior, acceptance of the disease still moves slowly where adolescents are concerned. Unfortunately, our society insists on believing that children cannot really become alcoholics or addicts, as they are "just too young."

During the past several years, increasing attention has been given to the number of young people developing addictions to alcohol and other drugs. The following facts, published through the National Council on Alcoholism and adapted from the "Kids Under the Influence" report, speak to the issue of adolescent chemical addictions and teenage alcoholism in a realistic and accurate manner.[8]

Alcohol-Related Facts

- Nearly five million of the twenty-three million Americans identified as problem drinkers are between fourteen and seventeen years old.
- The number-one killer of teens and young adults is alcohol-related highway death.

- Drivers between the ages of sixteen and twenty-four years old represent 20 percent of licensed drivers and less than 20 percent of total miles driven, yet account for 42 percent of all fatal alcohol-related crashes.
- Alcohol remains America's number-one drug problem among youth.
- Recent surveys indicate the first drinking episode today usually occurs around age twelve, in contrast to ages thirteen to fourteen in the 1940s and 1950s.
- Only 50 percent of fourth-graders surveyed knew that beer, wine, or liquor is a drug, compared to 87 percent who knew that marijuana is a drug.
- Every year two hundred to three hundred more young lives are lost as a result of alcohol poisoning in "chugalug" or drinking contests among adolescents.
- It takes less alcohol to produce impairment in youths than in adults.
- Children of Alcoholics have a four times greater risk of developing alcoholism than do children of nonalcoholics.
- By the time he is 18, the average American child sees an estimated 100,000 television commercials for beer.
- Teenage alcoholics comprise about 20 percent of the total alcoholic population in the United States.
- According to the spring 1987 *Weekly Reader*, more than one-third of the fourth-graders surveyed stated that kids their own age push each other to try beer, wine, or other liquor. Only 26 percent of those same fourth-graders thought there was any harm in drinking wine coolers, although 83 percent thought crack and cocaine were dangerous.

Other Drug-Related Facts

- 26 percent of kids who use marijuana first try it before high school.
- By their senior year in high school, half of all kids have used pot.
- Regular marijuana use impedes learning ability and motivation.
- Marijuana used on a regular basis decreases testosterone levels, which may have serious side effects for adolescents whose bodies are still developing.
- Marijuana impairs judgment and short-term memory for the adolescent user.
- Every day, five thousand Americans try cocaine for the first time, some of them adolescents.
- Almost always when kids use illicit substances, they regularly drink to adjust the effect of other drugs they take.
- From 70 percent to 95 percent of youths with cocaine and crack habits have histories of high-risk drinking, generally before the use of cocaine and crack.[9]

These facts are the observable and measurable results of adolescent alcoholism and other drug addictions. However, there are many symptoms that can be observed in the adolescent's behavior as early warning signs of a developing problem.

Roy was accustomed to alcohol being readily available at his home. His father had been drinking for as long as he could remember. Most nights his father drank until he passed out watching television, and Roy spent many nights alone while his mother worked evenings. Roy began to steal beer from the refrigerator downstairs after his father passed out. So far, no one

*had noticed the extra beer was gone because no one in
the family kept track of how much Roy's father drank.*

*Roy was thirteen years old when he began stealing
beers. He began by stealing one or two each night and
more recently was drinking four or five beers each
night. Roy enjoyed the feeling of confidence that the alcohol gave him. He would often sit and think about
what it would be like to live in another family or even
to live on his own. Roy and his dad had never spent
much time together, although Roy's dad promised that
they would go fishing or to a ballgame on a Saturday.
However, for some reason, they never did any of those
things together. His dad drank a lot on weekends, and
the fishing trips and ballgames were always planned for
the weekends. The pain of it all was a lot less intense
when Roy drank. He knew that he would never let his
drinking "get that bad."*

Roy—age 13

Some adolescents find that their experience with alcohol and other drugs is positive, even though they may
drink differently from their friends from the start.

*Chad recalls his first experience with alcohol as pos-
itive, even though his friends often teased him about being "the alcoholic of the group." The first time Chad
drank, he had three beers in an hour. His friends
wouldn't let him have any more that night because he
was already drunk.*

*To Chad, alcohol was an answer to many issues that
he had not been able to resolve himself. He often felt insecure and fearful inside but could not identify why.
With alcohol, Chad found that he could feel outgoing,
secure about himself, and less fearful of interactions
with people. It wasn't until Chad was arrested on a*

drunk-and-disorderly charge that he realized alcohol was no longer the answer for him. It was a painful realization.

Chad—age 16

Symptoms of Adolescent Chemical Dependency

During the teen years, which are generally characterized by moodiness, spurts of physical growth, and an ongoing identity search, the disease often remains unidentified while attempts are made to treat the erratic behavior of the adolescent. Yet the emotional and physical symptoms of the disease are often present in the young person.

Patti, a young woman with a multitude of problems, came into my office wearing a leather jacket, jeans, and boots. She appeared to be much older than her fourteen years, but there was also something vulnerable about her. She was angry, blaming her problems on school, her alcoholic father, and her "crazy" family situation. Patti had been in foster care, attended outpatient counseling, and lived in a residential treatment setting for adolescents with behavioral problems. Patti was not better. In fact, it appeared that things had gotten worse for her.

She looked tired and had circles under her eyes. She rarely stayed home at night, coming and going as she pleased, sometimes staying out all night. She admitted she drank beer and smoked marijuana, but said it wasn't a problem. Patti didn't connect any of her negative behavior or consequences to her chemical use. When I confronted Patti on the effects of her usage, she

*became angry and left my office. She said she did not
have a problem with chemicals.*

*I didn't hear from Patti again for six months or so.
She was on probation for truancy from school and lar-
ceny of a motor vehicle. Her probation officer called to
tell me that Patti was found on the street several hours
earlier and had almost overdosed on alcohol and barbiturates. She was in the adolescent psychiatric hospital,
in stable condition. When I arrived, Patti was sitting
and staring out the window. She looked scared and
hopeful at the same time. When I walked into her room,
she turned around and looked at me for a long time
without saying anything. When she spoke, she said, "I
know you think I tried to kill myself on purpose. I don't
know, maybe I did. I can only remember the first part of
the day. I can't remember what happened. Do you still
think I got a problem with alcohol and drugs?"*

Patti—age 15

The following list of symptoms encompasses both the
physical and emotional aspects of the disease.

Physical Symptoms

- Insomnia at night or excessive sleeping at inappropriate times, i.e., after school.
- Noticeable change in physical care of self; sloppy, un-
  kempt look.
- Unexplained weight loss or gain; change in eating
  habits; loss of appetite.
- Lethargic, dizzy, slurred speech and slowed reactions.
- Physically sick often, especially nausea and vomiting.
- Tremors or shaking of the hands, feet, or head (especially noticeable in the morning) signaling the beginning of withdrawal.

- Hyperactivity characterized by rapid speech and jerky movements.
- Watery eyes, persistent cough, droopy eyelids, and loss of short-term memory.
- Tired-looking, sallow complexion, and little direct eye contact with others.

Emotional Symptoms

- Oversensitivity to requests or neglect of simple tasks and duties.
- Changes in friends and meeting places.
- Loss of interest in hobbies, sports, or previously important activities.
- Secretiveness, withdrawal from others; lying frequently when unnecessary.
- Changes in grades at school; skipping classes; performance drop at school; "nodding off" in classes.
- Moodiness with increasing hostility, anger, and resentment toward others.
- Lack of follow-through with home and school responsibilities.
- An overall "I don't care" attitude toward life.
- Increasing physical and emotional withdrawal from family and previous friends.
- Inability to remember discussions held, particularly with family members.
- Lack of willingness to discuss family problems or come to any resolution for change.

Adolescent alcoholism and chemical dependencies seem to be much more frightening for adults than do other adolescent disorders. Most adults perceive the previously mentioned symptoms of chemical dependency as phases of adolescence. Misinterpretation of the behavior of the disease of adolescent chemical dependency has lessened due to increased education and awareness, but certainly it still exists.

For example, adults often seem to be relieved that a young person is "just using alcohol." Part of this attitude seems to come from the drug scare of the late 1960s and early 1970s when young people were experimenting with acid, marijuana, and "angel dust." Adults seem to sigh with relief and expect young people to experiment with alcohol, considered a much "safer" and more acceptable drug. Often families will introduce alcohol to their son or daughter to prevent the use of more harmful drugs, not realizing that alcohol is in fact the most harmful and widely abused drug in our society.

It is easy to see how alcohol has become a primary drug of choice among young people. Alcohol is easy to obtain, more acceptable, and seemingly less dangerous than other chemicals. In many states it is easy for young people to purchase beer and liquor. The number of adolescent alcoholics seems to increase each year.

Marijuana, cocaine, and speed rank as secondary drugs of choice for many adolescents. While the use of alcohol and drugs among young people may not disturb most adults, what is alarming is the increasing rate of alcoholism and drug dependency among today's youth. Just as alarming is the fact that children are now beginning drug use at much earlier ages.

Adolescents with the progressive disease of chemical dependency may possess one or all the components of the X-factor. Nearly 70 percent of the young people who develop this disease also have at least one alcoholic parent. Often the adolescent has not lived with the alcoholic parent due to divorce, death, or absenteeism. The environmental causes or origins of the disease seem to be much less significant than the actual genetic predisposition to the addiction. Young people with a genetic predisposition seem to use alcohol and other chemicals differently from the onset. They may experience memory losses as a result of their drinking or be able to tolerate large amounts of alcohol with seemingly little effect after only several months of active drinking and other chemical usage.

Some adolescents may not have an alcoholic parent, although alcoholism may exist in their paternal or maternal family tree. Other young people may begin using chemicals as a problem-solving technique. Still others may exhibit violent or aggressive personality changes from small amounts of alcohol and other drugs. Demands may be initiated by an inability to make friends, maintain satisfactory grades in school, or get along with parents. Chemical usage may allow adolescents acceptance by peers and the perceived ability to cope with adult expectations.

Amy used alcohol for the first time when she was thirteen years old. She recalls her first experience with alcohol as positive and liked the free feeling she got when she drank. She felt good inside, a feeling that was foreign to her. She intended to be very careful with her usage, because she didn't want to turn into a "burnout" like her sixteen-year-old brother, Tim. She was not going to use "drugs," just alcohol.

Amy used alcohol until she was fourteen years old and tried marijuana the same year. She also used cocaine when she was fifteen years old. Soon she was using alcohol daily before school and cocaine and marijuana at night. Her grades at school began to drop, and she no longer cared what she looked like. She was suspended from school for being drunk in class, and she didn't care.

She was finding increased relief for her problems in beer and cocaine. She felt as if she could handle anything and everything seemed better when she was using cocaine. Amy felt good when she used drugs, but she began to need more of the cocaine to get that same good feeling.

Amy often needed money to buy her cocaine and began to steal from her parents. She also withdrew money from her savings account but hid her savings book, hoping her parents wouldn't find out.

In June of that year Amy broke into a house that she walked by every day on her way to school. She had looked at the house often, and she knew the people who lived there were wealthy. She walked up to the sliding door by the side of the house, picked up a rock, and broke the glass. She reached in and opened the door. Once inside, she hurried to the bedroom and opened dresser drawers in search of money and jewelry. She heard a car pull up in the driveway and stopped abruptly. The people who lived there were home.

The family pressed charges against Amy for breaking and entering. She was placed in juvenile hall pending treatment in a chemical dependency program. She had been unaware that she could get into drugs this deeply. She had really believed that she was going to be different from her brother.

Amy—age 15

Many young people who begin using alcohol and other chemicals believe that their experience will be different. Their patterns of usage may differ, as may their choice of chemical; but what remains constant is their relationship with their chemical. In its early stages the relationship is positive and confidence-building. Most dependent adolescents will recall their first use of chemicals as a feeling of being "at home," a "this is it" kind of sensation.

Their duration of usage is often relatively short, consequences from their usage develop early on in the disease process, and attempts at quitting are invariably futile.

In the beginning of their dependencies, young people do not understand the memory losses, the high tolerance for alcohol and other drugs that they acquire quickly, nor the importance of chemicals in their life at such an early age. Nor do they understand the symptoms of the disease and the subtle personality changes that they are experiencing as the disease progresses. At this point in the disease process, life is fun, things are good, and their chemical usage is viewed as an activity that makes life "just a little bit better."

CHAPTER 2

The Progression of Dependency

Things do not continue to "get better" once an adolescent develops an addiction to chemicals and begins to progress through the stages of chemical dependency. This disease is progressive and will continue to progress unless arrested by abstinence from all mood-altering chemicals, including alcohol. The stages of progression are definable and observable in the adolescent.

Neither adults nor adolescents who begin using alcohol and other chemicals believe they will have a problem with handling drugs. Most adolescents have preconceived ideas of the nature of an alcoholic that usually have little to do with themselves. *Adults* are alcoholics, drink too much, and get drunk too often. Adolescents tend to see themselves as "just experimenting" with alcohol and chemicals, having a good time.

The media helps promote the adolescent's perception that alcoholism is an adult drug dependency issue. The adolescent with a serious chemical problem is rarely depicted. Great strides have been made by parent groups, schools, juvenile justice systems, and concerned community agencies in the identification of alcohol and drug dependencies in the young adult population. Yet the alcoholic or drug-dependent adolescent remains typically, an exception to the rule, a stereotype.

Jason fit the stereotype of a young man with a serious chemical health problem. He entered my office wearing blue jeans, a white T-shirt, and lots of metal around his neck. His face was hidden by his long hair, and he would not look me in the eyes for any length of time. He had been referred by his school for a chemical dependency assessment after being suspended three times for being either drunk or stoned at school.

Jason was obviously stoned during the assessment and had a difficult time answering my questions. His responses were disjointed and confusing. I got the distinct feeling that he thought his answers were very deep and philosophical. Through his drug-glazed eyes he looked confident, yet scared at the same time. He told me that he was on the first leg of his journey through life and that he was experiencing life as it came to him. Jason admitted that he had been doing acid regularly for the past six months and that acid only enhanced his journey through life. He was not the slightest bit interested in stopping his chemical usage.

As the assessment progressed, it became obvious that Jason was incapable of making a decision to get treatment for his chemical dependency. Later that same day, he was admitted to a detoxification unit to ensure a medically supervised and safe withdrawal from drugs. The locked unit housed young people like Jason who were at high risk of leaving treatment before detoxification from alcohol and drugs could be accomplished.

Jason—age 14

Adolescents, much like their adult counterparts, are not viewed as having a problem with drugs if they continue to function normally at school and at home. For years adult alcoholics have faced this stereotyping owing to misconceptions about the disease. Adolescents and adults with chemical health problems can often function for long periods of time without their chemical usage being noticed or identified as a problem. However, adolescents seem to be able to function for shorter periods of time with an active dependency.

Megan and her parents were quite indignant when the court referred her to the adolescent chemical dependency unit following her hearing. Megan, an attractive and extremely manipulative young woman, had run away from home for two weeks and incurred an informal charge of possession of marijuana, now pending in juvenile court. Her parents were concerned and more than willing to be involved in family counseling. However, both felt that this referral was a bit severe. Certainly Megan was somewhat involved with drugs, but she was not like the other young people in this unit who appeared to be "delinquents." Megan sat with an "I can't be bothered" look about her, silently agreeing with her parents.

It became clear that Megan controlled her parents and was accustomed to getting her own way. She was still in school and maintaining her grades after many confrontations with her parents. At home she set her own rules for curfews, coming home much later than her parents requested. However, she always had an excuse. Megan's parents could not believe that she could be in serious trouble with alcohol or drugs.

It was only after I had an opportunity to meet with Megan and her parents separately that some brief but significantly honest statements facilitated Megan's admission into treatment. Truths are difficult realities to face for anyone living with a dependent young person.

Megan—age 16

The disease, although certainly obvious in the chronic phase of dependency, is less conspicuous in its early stages. Dependent young people will do all they can to hide the extent of their usage from parents, which makes the disease even more difficult to identify. In essence, such individuals become experts at presenting a false image to the world, leading others to believe that alcohol and/or chemicals have not become an integral part of their life-style.

Stereotyping of both adults and adolescents with chemical health problems still occurs, especially in the perception of what a person with the disease looks like or does. Until recently, the drug-dependent adolescent has been characterized in much the same manner as a "skid row bum"—suffering from irreparable brain damage, drinking himself to insanity or death without any intervention in the disease.

The adolescent counterpart of the "skid row bum" is often characterized and referred to as a "burnout" by other adolescents. Concerned persons in the community may know this particular adolescent has a serious problem with alcohol and drugs, and some agencies may have even intervened to obtain professional assistance for the young person. Nevertheless, the adolescent continues to use chemicals destructively and is often seen around town either drunk or stoned. Some characteristics of drug-dependent youth are:

- Dropping out of school at age sixteen or younger.
- Involvement with the juvenile justice system, perhaps on probation for chemical-related offenses.
- A tired look, with poor, sallow complexion.
- Frequent drunkenness or "stoned" appearance.
- Believed to be dealing drugs.

An adolescent in the chronic stage of chemical dependency is easily identified. At this point in the disease, some irreparable brain and psychomotor damage has probably taken place.

Such a young person, although sad to observe, represents a minority of the dependent adolescent population. Most are found in school, on the football and basketball teams, on the cheerleading squad, on the honor roll. The various stages of the disease and the unique behavior of each adolescent seem to make it difficult to identify those who are developing a dependency on alcohol and other chemicals. Yet, once identified, the symptoms of the disease can alert parents and other adults to the problem.

Tony walked into the room of adolescent patients in the smoking lounge of the treatment setting and sat down. He tried to appear inconspicuous, but standing six-feet-two, he was noticed immediately by the other inpatients. Tony was on his high-school basketball team. Several of the young people who knew him asked him why he was coming to the treatment center. He replied that his parents thought that he had a problem with alcohol, but they usually overreacted to situations. Tony implied that his alcohol usage was not that big a deal.

Tony's father had called the chemical dependency unit two days before Tony was admitted. Tony had been arrested eight weeks before on his first drunk-driving charge and had spent the night in jail. He had promised his father that night that he would not drink and drive anymore. He had also promised that he would cut back on his drinking.

Two weeks later Tony's father had answered the phone to hear the emergency room staff tell him that Tony had been in an accident while driving his friend's car. Three of his friends were with him when he'd lost control of the car and flipped it three times. All four adolescents were bruised and cut up. None of them had any critical injuries, but all had suffered broken bones. That night in the emergency room, Tony had told his father that he hadn't meant to get drunk; he also had not meant to drive his friend's car. He promised that nothing like this would happen again. Tony's dad believed him.

Four days prior to Tony's admission on a Saturday night, Tony's father had received a call from the police. Tony had borrowed his friend's car to go to the store to buy some more beer and had been picked up for drunk driving. Tony's father let Tony sit in jail that entire night. As painful as it was for them, when Tony's father and mother went to pick Tony up from jail that next day, they had already decided that they would admit their son for inpatient treatment for his alcoholism.

At the jail, Tony looked at his parents in disbelief when they told him he would be going to treatment. He was angry that his parents were "overreacting" to his alcohol usage.

Tony—age 17

To an adult, the adolescent developing an addiction to alcohol and other chemicals may seem to be displaying both confusing and unpredictable behavior. Adults involved with an addicted adolescent seem to acknowledge the *behavior* accompanying the disease as the issue to be addressed, often the result of a lack of knowledge about the disease itself. Unpredictable and secretive behavior is to be expected. Adolescents developing an active dependency on alcohol and other drugs are in denial of their disease, as are those closest to them, including parents, teachers, and counselors.

*Jeff was an intelligent fifteen-year-old who was get-
ting C's and D's at school. His grades had dropped over
the past two years, and his attitude toward his teachers
had changed significantly. He was truant from school
often and had been observed drunk at school by several
teachers who cared about him and were concerned
about what was happening to him. Jeff had been suspended from school the day he had gotten angry and hit
his locker, breaking several bones in his hand. Jeff was
referred to a psychologist who diagnosed him as having
an acute problem with chemicals resulting in aggressive
and self-destructive tendencies. Jeff's parents became
increasingly concerned about their son's use of alcohol
and marijuana.*

*After the drunken episode at school, Jeff's father had
checked Jeff's room and found whiskey bottles hidden in
his closet and in the mattress of his water bed. Looking
around, Jeff's father had realized that his son's once
neat and clean room was now sloppy and disorderly. He
also realized that Jeff had not participated in family activities for months.*

*Jeff's father sat down on his son's bed and began to
think about Jeff. He discovered that he had many feelings about what was happening to his son. He barely
knew him anymore. He was confused and scared when
he recalled the past two years and his son's physical
and emotional deterioration. It seemed almost inconceivable that Jeff could be experiencing serious difficulties with alcohol and drugs.*

Jeff—age 15

Adolescent chemical dependencies are too often
viewed as symptoms of difficulties other than drug addiction. Attitudes about the period of adolescence tend to
further cloud the proper diagnosis of an alcohol or drug

dependency in a teenager. Attitudes such as "Kids will be kids" and "They are just going through a phase" can do more harm than good—the behavior changes accompanying an addiction are often misdiagnosed as a result of these attitudes. The adolescent's change in friends, appearance, and personal hygiene are too often perceived by adults as typical behaviors of youth. The accompanying personality changes of the young person, including disrespect for parental rules and authority figures, are viewed as rebelliousness and somewhat normal phases of development for all adolescents struggling with self-identity. Drug-dependent adolescents' behaviors are dictated by their disease and the reality that mood-altering chemicals have become a priority in their lives.

The adolescent seems to have an endless number of reasons to validate his use of alcohol and other chemicals—just like his adult counterparts. For example, the adult addict

- doesn't drink or use drugs before 5:00 P.M.
- never drinks or uses drugs in the morning.
- only drinks or uses drugs on the weekend.
- only drinks beer.
- only takes the pills the doctor has prescribed for depression.
- goes to work every day and brings home a paycheck.
- can quit anytime he wants to.

The adolescent, caught up in a maze of self-deception and rationalizations, will also list the reasons he can't possibly be an alcoholic or dependent on chemicals. After all, he

- doesn't use chemicals any more than his friends do.
- just enjoys getting a "buzz" now and then.

- only drinks beer.
- only drinks and gets high on weekends.
- still attends school.
- holds a part-time job.
- only uses marijuana.
- just likes to "party" and have a good time.
- can quit any time he wants to.

Chemical dependency continues to be a major health problem for both adults and young people. It is not of utmost importance what chemicals the adolescent uses or even how much. What is important is the relationship that the adolescent forms with his or her chemical of choice.

Friends

The relationship with alcohol and other chemicals that the young person forms early in his usage can be compared to that of a friend—but not just any friend. This friend is always there, a source of comfort, a best friend. For some young people the chemical may be the best friend they have ever had. Because of his initial experiences with the chemical, usually described as positive and remembered with fondness, the adolescent will continue to return to his chemical of choice despite the many negative consequences.

Angie became angry in the group when her peers challenged her denial of her alcoholism. She had admitted that she was a drug addict, but she would not acknowledge her other ongoing problem.

Angie had been in a car accident that she could not fully recall, as she had a memory lapse that evening while drinking. She remembered drinking the wine she had bought but had forgotten most of the evening of the car accident.

Angie had driven head-on into another car. She thought that she might have passed out at the wheel, but she couldn't remember exactly. She was injured and lost several of her front teeth in the accident. The man she had run into was in serious condition for over four days but was now in stable condition. When Angie discussed the accident, she honestly believed that she had not been drunk enough to cause a car accident. She had gotten high on marijuana and taken some downers that day and believed that had she not taken the other drugs, she would not have had an accident in the car. She still believed that she could handle alcohol.

Angie's blood alcohol content at the time of the accident was .21, an exceedingly high level. Most people could not even function, let alone drive a car, with an alcohol count that high. Angie clearly had a very high tolerance for alcohol, a definable symptom of the disease.

At her intake assessment, Angie had listed her drug of choice as alcohol. She simply would not believe that she would have to give up alcohol in order to live a healthy life. She remembered too many good times with alcohol.

Angie—age 14

"Euphoric recall"—the experience of remembering only the positive experiences with alcohol or other chemicals and the many good times and feelings associated with their usage—allows the adolescent to repress, deny, and minimize the negative aspects of chemical usage. The chemical will continue to be viewed as the solution, rather than the problem, as long as the adolescent can maintain his denial and rationalizations.

Addictions, characterized by compulsive use of a chemical despite damage in many areas, are very pow-

erful influences in the lives of drug- and alcohol-
dependent young people.

Chemical usage becomes the most important and
valued aspect of their life. Nonaddicted parents, teachers, and friends find this hard to believe. How could
anyone allow himself to be ruled by alcohol, marijuana,
or cocaine?

*Dawn had been attending family counseling sessions
with her parents for the past month. The focus of the
sessions would always seem to switch to Dawn's chemical usage, and she began to hate the counseling sessions. At the usual family session, her parents and the
counselor had planned an intervention on her destructive chemical usage. That evening Dawn learned that
she would be going into an inpatient treatment setting
for chemically dependent adolescents. Angry and defiant, Dawn agreed to go but stated that she intended to
leave as soon as her two weeks were up and to stay two
weeks only to placate her parents.*

*Returning home to get her clothes before entering
treatment, Dawn went upstairs to her room one last time.
She had some speed in her room and decided to take it
with her. No one would know. Besides, this place was
probably going to be a real drag and she might as well
have something to get her through. There was no way
that she was going to go two weeks without drugs. Dawn
took several pens out of her purse and unscrewed the
lids. She stuck the speed into the lids of the pens and
screwed the lids back on. She felt relieved that she would
have something with her in case "things got too tough."*

*When Dawn was admitted to the unit, her luggage
was checked for drugs as a matter of normal procedure.
The nurse asked for Dawn's purse and dumped it out on
the bed. As she began unscrewing the lids of the pens,*

*Dawn's face froze. The nurse calmly removed the am-
phetamines from each pen and replaced the caps.*

*Dawn decided at that moment that she didn't like the
nurse or this program or anything about this place. She
intended to leave as soon as she could figure out how.
But how could she go without her drugs?*

Dawn—age 16

The drug- and alcohol-dependent adolescent spends a
great deal of time thinking about, recalling, looking forward to, and planning the next chemical usage experience. In the disease, this is referred to as
"preoccupation." The adolescent's time is also spent lying about, covering up, and hiding his chemical usage.
This preoccupation with chemical usage, along with the
accompanying feelings of guilt and remorse, is rarely
verbalized to others but is always present and is a motivating factor in behavior.

*Kelly sat with her head down in the group while four
of her adolescent peers confronted her about a phone
conversation they had overheard. Apparently Kelly had
been talking to a friend about leaving treatment so that
the two of them could go and get loaded. Kelly had been
in the inpatient treatment setting for the past eleven days
and was leaving because she didn't agree with the re-
striction that the entire group had gotten over the weekend for negative behaviors. Her peers told Kelly that they
thought her excuse was just a cop-out. They asked her
how long she thought she would last if she went back to
drinking the way she was before she came into treatment.
They asked her how long she could drink a fifth a day
and still stay alive. They asked her why she didn't like
herself enough to finish treatment. As the questions continued, Kelly stared down at the carpet.*

At last she looked up at her peers and replied, "I can make it just fine. Besides, no one here really knows me." She stood up and walked out of the group to pack her bags and leave. What she didn't know was that the group knew Kelly better than she knew herself.

Kelly—age 14

The disease progression is increasingly visible as the chemical usage becomes more uncontrollable. Adolescents cannot predict, with any regularity, what their behavior will be once they begin to use chemicals. They cannot predict whether they will continue to drink and get in a car and drive, smoke another joint and get in a fight with a best friend, or do a line of cocaine and skip classes for the entire day. They cannot predict on any chemical-using occasion how the chemical will affect them.

The phases of chemical dependency are predictable, however, and although all of the described behaviors may not fit the dependent adolescent, the overall progression and resulting consequences vary only slightly from one adolescent to another.

The disease progression will continue, despite the adolescent's trying to quit or cut down on his usage for short periods of time, switching his chemical of choice or seeking help for the problems created by his ongoing dependency. The disease is primary in that it is the major source of the adolescent's problems and emotional deterioration.

Looking tired and defeated, Terry came into the assessment interview with his mother. Terry seemed apathetic, and his eyes looked heavy. He had smoked a joint at 11:30 A.M., and it was now 1:30 P.M. Terry said that he'd gotten high before coming to the chemical dependency assessment because he was embarrassed that he hadn't been able to make it on his own. Terry had been expelled from school and had lost all his credits for the past nine weeks of the school semester. His mother had kicked him out of the house when he refused to attend school, so Terry was staying at a friend's house. Terry was getting frightened about how quickly his drug usage was causing him seemingly uncorrectable problems. Looking pale and relieved, he agreed to enter treatment for his disease.

Terry—age 17

Often the adolescent's first drinking or drug-taking experience indicates that he has a much higher tolerance for alcohol and other chemicals than his friends do. He may be able to drink more and appear to be less affected by the chemical. He may experience memory losses during his first several drinking episodes. Personality changes may be visible, especially noticeable when a relatively quiet young person becomes violent and aggressive. All of the symptoms may be indicators of a potential or progressive problem with chemical usage.

Loss of control when using chemicals—a key factor in the identification of a problem—may not happen every time the adolescent drinks or uses chemicals but will become more frequent over time. Although the young person beginning his usage may fully intend not to get too drunk or too stoned, the result is often uncontrollable. Good intentions and self-deception lead the adolescent to believe that he will use only to the point of "feeling good" and "getting a buzz." The disease simply does not work that way. As his drug of choice becomes more addicting psychologically, the adolescent becomes caught in a vicious cycle of usage.

Dave broke down and cried when he talked about the pain that he had caused his parents. He hadn't meant to hurt them, nor had he realized how much they had been hurt by his continued chemical usage and its consequences. His parents often said that Dave was not listening, but he seemed to be hearing his parents today.

Dave listened quietly as his parents described his drunken behavior at home. He watched his father break down and cry when he described the night Dave had tried to get into a fist fight with him but couldn't stand up and kept falling down in the kitchen. Dave listened as his father described how he had held his son down until he'd passed out on the kitchen floor. Dave had not remembered that night; only fragments came back as he listened. Dave continued to cry silently as his parents described several other incidents that Dave did not remember. Dave had begun to listen.

Dave—age 15

Adolescents may use a number of different drugs simultaneously to heighten the drugs' effect, or they may ultimately settle on one or two drugs exclusively. When their drugs of choice are not available, they may switch to something else, then return to their original choice, primarily because of its emotional and psychological effects. Use of more than one chemical at a time will often speed up an addiction, causing the user to suffer consequences earlier than will his adult counterpart.

Mood-Altering Chemicals

Alcohol: Most adolescents will use alcohol in conjunction with the other drugs they become dependent upon. In fact, it is rare today to find a young person who becomes dependent only upon alcohol. Most will use a variety of drugs during their disease progression, often choosing alcohol first because of its easy availability. In fact, because of its easy access and social acceptance, many children will try alcohol before they try any other drug.

Marijuana: Marijuana, also known, among other terms, as "grass," "pot," "reefer," "herb," and "weed," is a widely used drug in the United States today, among both adults and adolescents. Chronic use of marijuana in an adolescent can delay development, interfere with short-term memory, learning, and comprehension, and slow the acquisition of social and problem-solving skills. Most adolescents who become heavily involved with marijuana become lethargic, display an inability to handle challenges, and lack basic direction and goals.[1] As marijuana becomes more potent, it also grows more expensive. Fifteen years ago an ounce of pot may have cost fifteen or twenty dollars, depending upon the grade purchased. Today an ounce of sinsemilla, the highest grade of marijuana available, can be as expensive as two hundred dollars per ounce.[2]

Cocaine: Cocaine is a stimulant, known for increasing heart rate and blood pressure. Several different types of cocaine are available to the adolescent user. The most common form is a white powder sold by the gram, half-gram, or quarter-gram. Cocaine powder is inhaled through the nose, a process known as "snorting." "Freebase," a purified form of cocaine that is heated with cocaine powder and other solvents, is smoked in a water pipe.

Cocaine gets to the brain quickly, giving the user a rush or euphoria, depending upon the manner in which it is used. If cocaine is smoked, it gives the user the most intense and immediate peak effect, usually in fifteen seconds. If cocaine is inhaled, the user feels the effects in about fifteen minutes. Cocaine use creates a feeling that "all is right with the world." Its high is followed by depression and craving because the drug depletes the brain's supply of such natural chemicals as norepinephrine and dopamine. Cocaine has become less expensive in recent years; what once cost the user one hundred dollars per gram can now be purchased for around fifty dollars per gram.[3]

Crack: Crack is one of today's most talked about drugs, particularly in relation to adolescent drug use. It is a kind of freebase cocaine that comes in the form of "rocks," ready to smoke. Crack is often smoked in a water pipe or applied to marijuana or tobacco cigarettes, called "fry daddies." At five to ten dollars per rock, it is a cheap drug to buy and one that kids can become addicted to in under two months. Crack is also economically seductive for kids since it promises them a "healthy income" if they become involved in the trade.[4]

Many adolescents begin to use cocaine and crack with little information about their highly addictive qualities. Because of the intensity of the cravings they engender, they are among the most addictive drugs in existence. Cocaine now accounts for a rapid acceleration of the disease progression in some adolescents. The full devastation that cocaine and crack addictions are bringing about in today's young people may not be truly felt for many years.

Hallucinogenics: Hallucinogenic drugs were very popular in the late 1960s and early 1970s with the introduction of peyote, mescaline, and, later, LSD. They seemed to die out around the late 1970s, then reemerged several years ago among adolescents, often becoming available when "acid rock" bands came into town. LSD, commonly known for producing hallucinations and causing "bad trips" or panic attacks, may sell for as little as five dollars per "hit."

Other hallucinogenic drugs, including peyote and mescaline, affect sensations and alter vision during use. Hallucinations may either be mild or overwhelming, depending upon the quality of the drug. Since almost all hallucinogenic drugs are smuggled in from abroad, it is virtually impossible to know the quality prior to usage.

PCP: PCP, also known as "angel dust," was developed as a surgical anesthetic for humans in the late 1950s. Its negative side effects, including visual disturbances, delirium, and extreme excitement in humans, eventually prohibited its use as an animal tranquilizer as well. PCP acts as a stimulant and depressant drug simultaneously. It is also a hallucinogenic drug that can cause the same panic attacks as LSD. PCP can produce violent behavior in the user, in addition to delusions and hallucinations. PCP use carries with it a high risk of organ and brain damage, making it one of the more dangerous drugs. Although some adolescents may experiment with or occasionally use PCP, it is not a popular drug, mainly because of its negative side effects.[5]

Amphetamines: There are several types of amphetamine, or stimulant, drugs available. Amphetamines, also referred to as "speed," are available in either pill or capsule form. Methamphetamine powder, known also as "crystal" on the streets, is snorted or injected. Crystal has gained popularity over the past several years with both adolescents and young adults. Its effects include hypertension, extreme anxiety, and insomnia, with some users staying awake for two to three days at a time. At a cost of approximately twenty-five dollars per gram, its inherent danger lies in the uncertainty about both its quality and its content.[6] Speed does just what its name implies: it speeds up the central nervous system, heartbeat, breathing, and blood pressure. Speed suppresses the appetite, making it a highly sought after drug for adolescent females trying to lose weight. Amphetamine drugs of all types are very addictive. Users of intravenous amphetamines are at increased risk of developing AIDS.

Designer Drugs: MDMA, also known as "ecstasy," comes in a powder form that can be either inhaled or injected, and in the form of capsules, which are taken orally. This drug acts as a depressant and mild hallucinogenic. MDMA was legal until the mid-1980s, when it was banned by the U.S. Drug Enforcement Agency. Because the drug is so new, not enough is known about its long-term effects. It may cause liver damage and also deplete a key chemical in the brain, serotonin. MDMA is known to cause brain damage in rats.[7]

Ice: Ice is recrystallized methamphetamine, a purer form of speed. This drug, also known as "glass," can be smoked and causes euphoria lasting anywhere from seven to thirty hours. Ice can lead to physical dependence and can also be fatal. Emergency room episodes involving ice in six cities rose 10 percent from 726 in 1985 to 1,523 in 1987. Deaths related to the use of ice rose 78 percent from 65 to 116 from 1985 to 1986. Though recovery from addiction to this drug is possible, rapid recovery is rare. Those in recovery can suffer from seizures, insomnia, and impaired judgment.[8]

Inhalants: Inhalant drugs popular among adolescents include typewriter correction fluid, glues, gases, paint thinners, and other household substances. These drugs tend to be more popular in rural areas, where kids do not have easy access to some of the drugs available in larger cities. They are also popular among the younger users, those between eleven and thirteen years old. Long-term inhalant use can be very destructive to the growing adolescent; organ damage, memory impairment, seizures, neurological damage, and brain damage can result. Many adolescents who begin an addiction to inhalant drugs do irreversible damage to their bodies.

The drugs available to adolescents are often used simultaneously, producing a synergistic effect and speeding up the potential of addiction. The disease progresses in stages, with the adolescent gradually losing control of his life.

The disease of chemical dependency progresses in a vicious downward spiral unless arrested by abstinence from all mood-altering chemicals. For adolescents with the progressive disease of chemical dependency, abstinence is the only answer.

The *early phase* of the disease consists of

- an increase in the amount of chemical usage and frequency of usage.
- inconsistent behavior with evidence of a low frustration tolerance.
- an apparent change in the quality of home and school life, including neglect of both home responsibilities and class attendance and increased sleepiness in the classroom and at home.

- change in friends, grades, and personal appearance.
- decrease in the ability to stop chemical usage.

The *crucial* or *acute phase* consists of

- changes in moods, swinging from elated to depressed and back again.
- decrease in or dropping out of extracurricular activities.
- increase in absenteeism and not following through on home guidelines.
- disciplinary problems at home and in school.
- deterioration in personal hygiene and appearance.
- legal difficulties.
- increased need for usage of chemicals.
- loss of control with usage occurring on a consistent basis.
- increased association with peers from the drug subculture.
- short-lived attempts at quitting.

The *chronic phase* is characterized by

- physical, mental, and emotional deterioration.
- daily chemical usage and lengthy "highs."
- dropping out of or no interest in school.
- impaired thinking and loss of memory.
- exhausted alibis or excuses and desire for help.
- admission of defeat with chemical usage.

Once the adolescent begins to progress through the phases of chemical dependency, he often displays an inability to address issues honestly and adamantly denies any problem with his chemical usage. He becomes an expert at manipulating adults. He will present other problems as the cause of his difficulties. The dependent adolescent will continue to progress through the phases of the disease unless identification occurs and steps are taken to arrest the disease.

Greg sat with his arms crossed over his chest while he answered the questions during the chemical dependency assessment. He had just been arrested on his second drunk-driving charge. He and some friends had taken their senior skip day and Greg had been driving when he was stopped by the police. His blood alcohol content was .15 when the police tested him.

Greg did not believe that his alcohol usage was serious enough to be treated in an inpatient treatment setting. He indicated that he couldn't come into treatment anyway, because he had to work to pay off his fines, which now totaled $1,000. Greg planned to go to college in the fall and only had three months to "get his act together," as he described it.

Greg told me that he didn't intend to get drunk again. He would simply become a better judge of when to stop drinking. He did not intend to quit, but he did intend to cut back a little bit.

Greg became agitated and began looking at the clock. He had to be somewhere in fifteen minutes. He would try AA meetings, but he didn't really need them because only people who were physically addicted to alcohol needed AA.

As Greg shut the door behind him, I doubted that he'd quit drinking until he saw that he had no other options. I hoped that he would have another chance at treatment for his disease.

Greg—age 17

Addictions to chemicals and alcohol are often identified as the primary problem only after other alternatives to treating the behavioral symptoms of the disease have been exhausted. It is unusual to find a young person who has not been involved with a variety of treatment modalities, including visits to outpatient counselors and psychiatrists for other problems prior to treatment for the addiction. Improper diagnosis generally results in a continuation of chemical usage and the negative effects of usage at school, at home, and in other areas of the adolescent's personal life. These consequences prolong the young person's association with a life-style of chemical usage. The adolescent continues in a pattern of self-destruction as his disease progresses.

Few adolescents suffer the same consequences as adult addicts, who through long years of chemical usage are much more likely to suffer insanity, or "wet brains." Some adolescents, however, do end up in state hospitals as a result of their usage. Severe organic damage to brain cells may have occurred, and the young adult may be able to function only with assistance from professional caretakers. This prognosis seems to be particularly true for those teenagers who have used gasolines, glues, paints, and other inhalants for extended periods of time. The damage done by these drugs is irreparable and, in most cases, irreversible.

As inconceivable as it may seem, many adolescents will die as a result of their undiagnosed dependencies on alcohol and other chemicals. Deaths that are drug-related, however, are not always recorded as such. Suicides, in particular, can often be linked to heavy alcohol and other chemical usage. Automobile deaths among teenagers are occurring frequently, usually as a result of drunk driving. Accidental deaths (including drownings and chemical overdoses) can be linked to adolescent chemical dependencies. Yet many of these chemical-related deaths are never listed as such.

The following statistics from the National Council on Alcoholism are proof that in some cases the consequences of chemical addictions for this age group are irreversible:

- Life expectancy in the United States is increasing for every age group except adolescents, where drinking is playing an ever larger role.
- The number-one killer of teens and young adults is alcohol-related highway deaths.
- According to the National Highway Traffic Safety Administration, each year more than six hundred children below age thirteen killed in highway accidents had significant levels of alcohol in their blood, two-thirds of them as high as the legal levels for adult intoxication.
- Approximately ten thousand young people aged sixteen to twenty-four are killed each year in alcohol-related accidents of all kinds, including drownings, suicide, violent injuries, homicides, and injuries from fire.[9]

Denial runs deep for the teenager with an addiction. The consequences they suffer in arrested developmental tasks may not become completely clear until they have been sober for some time.

CHAPTER 3

The Dependent Adolescent

Adolescence is a tumultuous time, filled with conflicting emotions and confusion about oneself in relation to the rest of the world. Adolescence also signifies the completion of certain stages of development and, with this resolution, a greater ability to know oneself and one's own value system.

According to renowned psychiatrist Erik Erickson, these tasks occur in stages of development. How well a child does with one stage will determine his ease or discomfort in completing the next.[1]

Adolescence is a time of identity crises, with certain tasks moving the adolescent closer to adulthood and helping him to assume greater responsibility for his own actions and behavior. These tasks, in summary, include

- **Developing One's Individuality** The adolescent explores the question "Who am I?" while testing his ever-changing self-concept. Teenagers who experience difficulty with this task will be particularly susceptible to peer pressure, whether positive or negative. This fragile task is difficult for many adolescents and involves finding an inner comfort level to express individual values and preferences.
- **Forming Commitments** The adolescent experiments with various cultures and people, often through par-

ticipation in the adult work world. The essence of the
task of forming commitments is to allow the adolescent to experience accountability for his actions and
for the impact which he has on others.

- **Outgrowing Types of Egocentrism** Two main types
of egocentrism are usually present in an adolescent,
the feeling that he is often on stage and a type of psychological loneliness. The first type involves self-
involvement and includes concern about the
responses he receives from others in relation to his
appearance and personality. The second involves a
sense of immortality and a feeling that "bad things
will never happen to me." Both tasks are central to
the adolescent and must be completed in order for the
adolescent to fully understand the consequences of
his actions and behaviors.

- **Reevaluating Values** Adolescents will question adult
values, which is a necessary part of their growth and
development. Their peer group becomes a natural
source of information for decision-making and value
formation. As they move through this task, they determine what is important to them. They may also
look to adults to model behavior they would like to
emulate. The modeling of appropriate behaviors and
values will often be the job of parents, teachers, and
other significant adults.

- **Separation and Autonomy** This is one of the most
difficult tasks for young people, as they begin to
move outside their immediate family to incorporate
values, friendships, and opinions. This move toward
separation and autonomy from family will often create extreme conflict for parents. Although necessary
to growth, this task is often accompanied by pain for
the adolescent and his parents.

- **Experiencing Physical Sexual Maturity** This task,

usually occurring between the ages of twelve and sixteen years, initiates a range of feelings for the young person who, biologically, is undergoing tremendous change. Both males and females begin to assess the world around them and their part in that world as sexual beings. This assessment will affect both their peer and their adult relationships, often producing a sense of awkwardness about their developing bodies.

Adolescents who become harmfully involved with chemicals arrest their growth in these stages of development. They do not move appropriately from one stage to the next as their life goals become clouded by their addiction. Those from alcoholic or other dysfunctional families may not have completed some basic childhood tasks, such as learning to trust, having grown up in inconsistency and chaos. Some adolescents reveal these voids in development by their attempts to problem-solve with insufficient skills or tools.

While adults may suffer tangible losses as a result of chemical addiction, the adolescent's losses are seen in lack of psychological maturity. For an adult, the loss of job, home, spouse, car and driver's license, and physical health are the expected results of progressive addiction. Indeed, these losses are often the very motivators that enable an adult to seek help. The consequences of the adolescent's harmful involvement with alcohol and other drugs are visible in other ways.

Intellectually, many young people display arrested development and retain only minimal knowledge and comprehension of the material presented to them in the classroom and during related educational experiences. Their grades have most likely dropped or fluctuated as their interest in academic learning has decreased. Drug-dependent adolescents may continue to attend classes but be high or drunk at school. Their commitment to education has most likely become insignificant as their chemical usage has become more important to them.

Many young people who are dependent on chemicals may be labeled as incorrigible or troublemakers at school. Some may keep high grades at school but have noticeable personality changes. Lack of interest may be observed by both teachers and parents.

Adolescents with learning disabilities are often placed in classrooms for the emotionally impaired because of poor grades, disciplinary problems, and short attention spans in the classroom. These disabilities in learning, although often caused by other agents, can be the result of chemical health problems. Once the young person becomes chemical free and returns to healthier levels of functioning, the need for such a specialized study program may diminish.

Some adolescents may have high peer allegiance needs and attempt to minimize their intelligence to gain acceptance.

"Yeah, I've got an I.Q. of 135 or so they tell me from my testing. I can learn stuff pretty fast, but I've been in special ed for the past year and usually go to school buzzed and then get high once I get there because it's so boring. Besides, my friends would think I was weird if I acted smart all of the time."

Bruce—age 15

The dependent adolescent, contrary to the stereotype presented earlier, may be very intelligent and able to study less than other students while still maintaining a passing grade point average. In response to pressure from parents and teachers about a drop in grades, some addicted young people may be able to raise their grade point average in a relatively short time. However, once the pressure has been lifted, the grades will usually drop again as chemical usage takes priority.

This is similar for adult drug-dependent and alcoholic employees who experience problems on the job and will briefly pull together their work performance after a warning from their employer. The dependent adolescent's difficulties will often show up early in school with unexcused absences, tardiness, and a drop in performance. The adolescent may appear to be doing much better at school after a warning is issued from teachers or parents, but, like his adult counterpart, this improvement is usually short-lived.

Some adolescents, although very intelligent, have lost significant educational learning as a result of their dependency. For some, unexcused absences have resulted in suspensions from school and, in more severe cases, expulsion. Credits may have been lost, as have entire years of school. Intellectual development has been arrested, and thinking processes have been dulled by drugs and alcohol. Important academic learning has not taken place. The drug-dependent adolescent will have some catching up to do in intellectual growth and development.

Emotionally, the adolescent's development and growth may stop at the onset of his chemical usage. If an adolescent begins using chemicals at age thirteen and does not become abstinent from chemicals until fifteen, he will still think, behave, and attempt to solve problems on a thirteen-year-old's emotional level. The young person who has been medicating and numbing feelings of anger, sadness, or fear with chemicals has not developed the tools to face life's problems and situations chemical free. The dependent adolescent will seek an "easy way out" if given the choice: using chemicals to cope with the many problems of life seems less risky than facing the sometimes painful emotions of life's ups and downs. Honesty about feelings becomes threatening and frightening for the dependent adolescent, as does the ability to communicate those feelings.

"I don't know what I feel, but it sure isn't very good. Sometimes I just guess at the feeling, because it all becomes a big knot inside my stomach and I get confused. Like the last time that I drank a lot, I woke up the next day with a sick feeling inside because I couldn't remember a lot of the night before. The night all just ran together, so I tried to remember only the funny things that happened. But I knew that I had another blackout, and I wondered if I had made a real jerk of myself again. Sometimes I think I can handle my alcohol, but lately I don't know. I do know that I don't like this feeling of confusion now that I'm not getting high anymore."

Jim—age 16

The adolescent with a chemical addiction loses touch with his emotions and is increasingly unable to separate his dishonesty from real emotions and feelings. Parents, in particular, seem to experience the frustration and sadness caused by an addicted adolescent's lies and untruths.

"The first time I caught Cathy in a lie I didn't think that much about it. I guess all kids lie from time to time, and although I was concerned, I thought she had learned how upset I got about her lies to me. I soon discovered that Cathy was lying to me about many things, including her drug usage. I found marijuana in her

makeup purse in the bathroom and was angry and shocked. I guess deep down inside I knew that something was wrong with Cathy, but I didn't want to face it."

Joan
Parent

Chemical dependency allows young people to medicate their feelings and experience a false sense of euphoria. As their disease progresses, they will need more of the chemicals to produce the same euphoric feeling. This need will increase as they continue to blame people, places, and things outside of themselves for their resentments, angers, and fears.

"Jeff and I began having disagreements over rules and his using the car. He was unreasonable and would not listen to my concerns about his drinking and driving. He would get angry and call me names that shocked me. Most of the time, after one of our fights, he would slam the door and leave the house. I never knew where he was going or when he would be back. I began to feel like I was losing control and that I had no impact on Jeff anymore. He seemed to do as he pleased despite my yelling, screaming, and grounding him from the car and all activities. Things got worse and I actually began to dread his coming home because I knew there would probably be a fight. Then I would feel guilty for thinking that way about my own son. I didn't know that Jeff had a disease that was slowly destroying him and our family at the same time. Now that Jeff is sober, I look back and can't believe that we lived that way for such a long time. I never want to live like that again."

Bill
Parent

Emotionally, adolescents with an active addiction become increasingly resentful and angry toward the significant people in their lives, especially parents. They will insist that if their parents would just "get off their back" and "quit hassling" them, everything would be fine. Their emotional responses become unpredictable as they quickly fluctuate from happy to sad and back again. As their disease progresses, their mood swings become more observable and difficult to explain.

Important emotional growth is arrested as their disease progresses and they become increasingly difficult to live with and communicate with on an emotional level. The long-term effects of an addiction on adolescents who are developing emotionally and psychologically can be observed in an overall lack of attention to and interest in emotional health and well-being. Their need to focus on people, places, and things outside themselves to feel good indicates their lack of knowledge about how to care for themselves emotionally. (Those from alcoholic families usually had no adult models to teach them how.) For many, this realization and the growth steps they must take in order to "catch up" with others becomes one of the most painful tasks of sobriety.

Physically, the dependent adolescent has most likely experienced an acceleration in the phases of his disease progression due to the physical growth processes of adolescence and his simultaneous use of more than one chemical. Both factors will speed up addiction. Many adolescents are in the crucial or chronic phase of dependency before identification of their usage problem is made.

The multiple physical consequences of chemical usage are evidenced by the more serious beginnings of liver diseases, loss of short-term memory (particularly evident in adolescents who excessively use marijuana), and various physical scars and injuries resulting from falls and automobile accidents. Some adolescents while under the influence of chemicals may carve names or mottoes on their arms and hands, signaling self-destructive tendencies. This self-mutilation becomes a symptom of the self-destructive nature of the disease of alcoholism and drug dependencies. Suicide attempts among the chemically dependent population in general are more frequent than among the average population. It is estimated that perhaps 40 percent of the chemically dependent population will attempt suicide at some point in their disease. This figure in part explains the high suicide rate among today's teenage population.

Many adolescent females, as with adult drug-dependent women, face specific problems as a result of their addictions. Females with drug dependencies often encounter gynecological problems because their chemical usage affects the monthly hormonal changes of their menstrual cycles. They may also suffer the consequences of decisions to become sexually active made while under the influence of chemicals. Many of these adolescent females may become pregnant, which with subsequent continued use of chemicals may produce children with fetal alcohol syndrome.

Fetal alcohol syndrome, officially identified in the United States in 1973, is a pattern of mental, behavioral, and physical birth defects in babies born to women who drink heavily during pregnancy. FAS is characterized in the infant by both prenatal and postnatal growth deficiencies, including facial malformations, central nervous system dysfunction, and varying degrees of major organ system malformation. FAS is among the three leading known causes of birth defects and is the only preventable one among the three. In 1981 the surgeon general of the United States issued a health advisory recommending that pregnant women abstain from alcoholic beverages and also be aware of the content of foods, beverages, and medications that they ingest.[2]

Actual physical detoxification from alcohol and other chemicals seems to be less uncomfortable for young people than for their adult counterparts. Both adolescents and adults, however, are strongly encouraged by most professionals in the field to undergo a medically supervised detoxification treatment program in the event of withdrawal side effects.

The effects of withdrawal in adolescents show up in behavior patterns and moods. Erratic behavior and some mild depression, lasting anywhere from several days to three weeks depending upon the extent and duration of the usage, can be expected from dependent adolescents. Cloudy thinking processes, high levels of anxiety, and mood swings are normal for an adolescent withdrawing from chemicals, as are angry outbursts and self-imposed isolation from people. Each adolescent seems to detoxify in a manner unique to his own body chemistry. However, for some young people, detoxification from alcohol and drugs can be dangerous medically. This seems to be especially true for those addicted to alcohol and barbiturates, a dangerous combination for persons of any age.

Dennis, a sixteen-year-old who was heavily involved in alcohol and barbiturates was unaware that he had become physically dependent on these chemicals. He had tried to quit drugs about six months before, but after only one week he was using heavily again.

One week in March, Dennis made his second attempt

to quit using alcohol and downers. His parents left on a Friday evening for a weekend out of town to attend an activity with friends, and Dennis stopped using that same night.

Saturday was much worse than Friday evening for Dennis. He was physically sick and weak as he craved the chemicals he was trying to avoid. He ate little, slept most of the day, and began to hallucinate late Saturday evening, seeing bizarre animals and scary visions that he knew were not real.

When Dennis awoke on Sunday morning, he felt strange but was determined not to take any alcohol or downers. When his parents arrived home at one o'clock that afternoon, Dennis was in convulsions on the living room floor. Shocked and confused, his parents rushed him to the emergency room. Dennis was in full withdrawal.

Over the previous year and a half, Dennis had become increasingly dependent on his chemicals. He had been drinking and using speed daily but often used downers at night to get to sleep.

He was not aware that quitting would be so painful. He did not understand his addiction. Dennis was admitted to a detoxification room in the alcoholism unit at 2:30 P.M. He was placed on vitamin therapy, and doctors and nurses closely supervised his withdrawal process. Within seven days Dennis had gained seven pounds and was feeling better physically and emotionally.

Upon admission to an adolescent chemical dependency inpatient unit, Dennis acknowledged that he had a serious problem with alcohol and drugs and that he wanted to quit using. He honestly could not remember how the whole thing had gotten so serious. He thought that he could quit on his own. At last he seemed to be ready for treatment of his disease.

Dennis—age 16

Although most young people do not experience such a dramatic withdrawal process from chemicals, adolescents who become involved in a harmful pattern of dependency on alcohol and chemicals are always vulnerable to the physical consequences of their usage. For most, the physical damage caused by their addiction is treatable and will reverse once the addiction has been arrested and they are actively involved in a recovery program addressing their emotional and physical health. Some of the unlucky ones, however, will suffer from the beginning stages of liver disease, pancreatitis due to damage of the stomach lining, diabetes, low blood sugar or hypoglycemia, or other unreversible physical diseases.

Most adolescents have a distinct advantage, however; they are young and energetic and have the capacity to bounce back and enjoy physical health once they discontinue their use of all chemicals. Eventually the color returns to their complexions and they gain weight indicating the restoration of balance in their sleeping and eating habits.

Spiritually, dependent adolescents can be considered bankrupt. They have not had the life experiences or the exposure to healthful alternatives to help them identify what gives meaning to their lives. Their development has been arrested spiritually as their chemicals have become, in a sense, their false gods. Many adolescents have turned off to the entire concept of organized religion and view God as punishing and negative. After all, they are in the mess they are in because of their God, whom they may have bargained with to make things better. And obviously God is nonexistent or they would not be in this mess with their lives, right?

Many adolescents beginning their recovery process conceive of God as punitive and guilt-invoking. Alternatively, they may not believe that a power greater than themselves can exist, given all the negative circumstances in their lives.

Many people confuse the spiritual aspect of recovery with religion and believe that Alcoholics Anonymous and other spiritually based self-help programs are "Bible thumpers," pushing God and religion down the throats of recovering individuals. In essence, any person involved in a harmful dependency becomes caught up in trying to control and manage his own life and affairs, with little success. This is believed to be one of the major symptoms of the disease of chemical dependency. Attempts to quit using and to make one's life better have been futile without a spiritual-based program of recovery. The dependent adult or adolescent becomes an expert at trying to control his disease and the people, places, and things around him. Those living with the drug-dependent person become just as expert at trying to control the dependent person's usage and consequences. The only answer and viable solution seems to lie in giving up the unsuccessful attempts at control and turning to a power greater than themselves to return all parties to sanity and a healthful orientation to life.

Some young people have turned off to the concept of a Higher Power and made overt statements to society about their nonbelief in God. Some chemically involved adolescents have become involved in Satan worship and occult practices—behavior that is often bizarre and frightening to adults involved with them on any level. And that is the point. The reaction from adults is often what the adolescent is looking for. This phenomenon is exemplified in some young people's fascination with certain rock groups that purport to practice devil worship onstage.

Dependent adolescents rarely accept the concept of a power greater than themselves as a positive force in their lives. Major learning in this area of their recovery will be necessary for wellness and a return to emotional and spiritual health. Substantial spiritual development will most likely come about with their own self-exploration and identification of what gives meaning to their lives.

Ana was a bright, attractive sixteen-year-old who expected the world to revolve around her needs and desires. She was continually miserable waiting for this to happen. All of her attempts to manipulate and control her external environment were futile and caused her more difficulties than she was able to see clearly. Ana's temper tantrums, which used to work at home, did not work at the inpatient treatment center for drug-dependent adolescents. She would become increasingly hostile and aggressive if others did not respond in the manner that Ana wanted them to. She had no spiritual program to fall back on as she became frantic trying to change other people and get them to see things her way.

Ana began to apply the basic concepts of her AA program to her daily life and to verbalize the concepts of "Let go and let God" so often heard around AA tables. She began to exhibit a mature and rational approach to life that would aid in her recovery process from alcohol and other drugs. It was difficult learning for Ana to realize that she really had no control over other people, places, or things.

Ana—age 16

Spirituality can be seen in the manner that a dependent adolescent approaches life. It is a beautiful and rewarding experience to see an adolescent begin to apply the basic concepts of the AA program to his daily life.

Tommy, an argumentative and negative young man when he first entered treatment, began to use the philosophy of spirituality in his daily life. He became more positive and began to change his way of thinking about the circumstances that life dealt to him.

Tommy sat in my office one day with his sweat clothes on and asked question after question about the concept of a power greater than himself. He seemed to want concrete answers to the slogans of Alcoholics Anonymous and asked me what each slogan specifically meant. The one Tommy particularly liked was "One day at a time." Tommy began to apply that philosophy to his daily life. He once described to me how he used to wake up mornings and begin drinking before school began. In fact, it was the first thing he did in the morning. He seemed to feel that the days were all the same when he was using. He seemed relieved when he said, "Yeah, I understand what that means now, 'cause I never thought that way before. I know that AA tells us to take one day at a time. Before I came into treatment, I used to take two days at a time or sometimes even more if things were really bad. I guess that life would be a lot easier if everybody just took one day at a time. Don't you think so?"

Tommy—age 14

The consequences of their usage may vary, but the themes present in most adolescent drug-dependent and alcoholic persons remain constant. Their spiritual development is sadly lacking, and the acceptance of a power greater than themselves offers them both hope and serenity.

Legally, an adolescent may enter the juvenile justice system for obvious charges related to his dependency. Legal ramifications may occur in any phase of the disease and should be treated as warning signs or "red flags." A drunk-driving charge for an adolescent should be taken just as seriously as the same charge for an adult. At the same time that there is increasing emphasis on stiffer penalties for drunk-driving charges, regardless of the driver's age, these arrests are becoming more frequent among teenage drivers. A young person charged with possession of alcohol and other mood-altering substances may have either an impending problem with chemicals or an already out-of-control usage problem.

Some less obvious charges, such as breaking and entering or check forgery, may also relate to the adolescent's chemical usage. For example, an adolescent may be breaking the law because he needs money to purchase alcohol and other chemicals.

Juvenile court systems have had to rapidly adjust to the number of adolescents processed through the legal system for drug-related charges. Many juvenile justice systems are now skilled at identifying chemical dependency, while others remain uneducated and attempt to address only the delinquent behavior of the adolescent through incarceration and other punitive measures. Although adolescents certainly need to take responsibility for their behavior, they also need treatment for their disease. This lack of education in many juvenile justice systems will often result tragically in the adolescent becoming entrapped in the court system with repeated charges and frequent referrals to juvenile detention centers. No marked or lasting beneficial behavioral change results from incarceration for adolescents with addictions to chemicals, since it does not treat the disease. Many adolescents referred to adult court at the age of seventeen, after repeated juvenile offenses, are dependent young people whose disease progression has been misdiagnosed.

"The first time I was arrested I was fifteen years old. I was at a party with a bunch of my friends. When the police came to break up the party, I decided to take them all on and tell them exactly what I thought of them. I was arrested for drunk and disorderly conduct. That was just the beginning of my involvement in the court system. I was in juvenile hall once and was on probation from fifteen years old until I was seventeen. I guess you might say that I had to learn the hard way. I didn't go through treatment for my alcoholism and drug addiction until I was almost nineteen years old. Looking back, I can see that I drank to get drunk. I just wasn't the kind of guy who sat down and had a couple of beers to get mellow. I liked to pick fights and "get rowdy" when I drank. Now, I know that my aggressive behavior was just a part of my disease. Since I went through treatment and started going to Alcoholics Anonymous and Narcotics Anonymous meetings, I've seen a lot more kids coming into the program. I've started to sponsor a couple of the teenagers who come to AA. I figure if I can help a kid who's having troubles, I'm gonna give it my best shot. I guess I just hope that no kid has to go through all of the pain that I went through before I got to AA."

Steve—age 20

Even when young people have the chance to learn from a man like Steve, they may believe that they will be different. It is the typical alcoholic dilemma of their ongoing denial system. They get into trouble with the law and drink again anyway, believing that the next time will be different.

"I broke into a doctor's office one night after I'd been drinking, to steal some pills. I was doing downers a lot then and didn't think I'd get caught. Looking back, I guess the story really is kind of funny. I've told it at AA meetings and everybody has laughed, including me. That night I had been drinking and had gotten high and had decided that I wanted to do some downers. I felt a little burned out and kind of sick from all of the beer I had drunk, so I lay down on the couch for a minute in the doctor's office until I felt a little better. I fell asleep or passed out, I guess. Can you believe it? I was asleep on the couch inside the doctor's office I'd broken into when the cops found me!"

Joe—age 18

Sometimes, involvement with the legal system— probation and court involvement—may serve as the turning point for young people in the acceptance of their drug addiction and alcoholism.

Sexuality issues become clouded for young adolescents who are involved in a harmful dependency. Most adolescents will be just starting to relate to the opposite sex, questioning their own values and decision making in the area of sexuality; but the dependent adolescent makes fewer conscious and well-thought-out choices concerning his decision to become sexually active.

The young chemically dependent adolescent may enter into a sexual relationship while "under the influence" and later feel an additional burden of guilt and shame. This seems to be especially painful for the young person who was in a blackout, or temporary memory loss, while drinking and cannot remember parts of the evening before. Decisions to become sexually active while drunk or stoned only intensify the dependent adolescent's poor self-esteem.

For some dependent adolescents, sexual activity can be a bargaining tool to obtain drugs and alcohol. Although this may be shocking to some parents and counselors, it is a means of survival for the young addict.

"I didn't know the guy very well, but I had seen him at a few parties before. He seemed to really like to have a good time and to party, and I liked that. He was eighteen and could buy beer, so I thought, Why not? I knew if I had sex with him that he would buy me some beer, and I really felt like getting loaded that night. I really didn't think that much about it at the time. But, I feel pretty crummy about myself now."

Tracy—age 16

Young males, as well, may enter into relationships and, in some cases, homosexual relationships, solely to obtain drugs. The resulting embarrassment and confusion will tend to force the young male addict to remain silent rather than risk rejection by sharing his experiences. Yet identification of this kind of sexual activity as it relates to an ongoing harmful dependency on chemicals is necessary for self-acceptance and understanding of the disease. Unless the many feelings of remorse, guilt, and shame are worked through, the dependent male may carry fears of homosexuality into the recovery process, causing negative effects on relationships with both males and females. He must be able to explore his sexual preferences and begin to address his own sexuality, as well as the chemical addiction.

Some young people who become dependent on alcohol and other chemicals have been victims of incest. Incest is usually a subject that the adolescent will avoid at all costs because of the shame and feelings of self-blame associated with this sensitive issue. Incest seems to occur with frequency in families where there is one actively drinking parent, either a biological parent or stepparent. Incest between brothers and sisters also occurs, especially when both siblings are involved in alcohol and drugs. The most commonly reported incest occurs between daughters and their biological fathers or stepfathers. Incest often occurs in families with chemical-abuse histories and further complicates the "family secrets" in familial relationships.

Incest is both overt and covert in nature. Overt incest is more easily identified through actual physical and genital contact initiated by the parent or the stepparent. Covert incest is more difficult to define; although there is no actual inappropriate physical contact, the relationship tends to be incestuous, particularly on an emotional level. This again seems to be particularly true between fathers and daughters or stepfathers and daughters. The daughter will often assume the role of the wife within the home on an emotional level.

Covert incest, in these cases, seems to put the daughter in an awkward and unhealthy position in that she is often expected to meet the emotional needs of the father or stepfather and ultimately receives little of the direct parenting she needs for her own emotional growth.

"I never told anyone about my stepfather approaching me sexually because I felt so guilty about it. Once, when I finally did say something to my mom about it,

she didn't say too much. I told her that he was always walking into my room when I was dressing, and I felt uncomfortable about it. She told me to wear a robe. I also told her how he would come into my room late at night after he'd been drinking and tell me all of his problems. I didn't want to hear about the problems that he was having because I felt sad and sorry for him and there was nothing I could do about them anyway. But I always sat and listened to him. I wanted to fix things and make it better for him, but I couldn't. He never touched me or anything like that, but I was always cautious when I was around him. I sometimes wished that he and my mom had a better relationship."

Jenny—age 17

Unresolved feelings of guilt and shame stemming from overt incest, and the confusion and anguish of being placed in the role of surrogate wife in covert incest situations, further hampers the adolescent's growth and development in areas of sexual identity and value clarification. In most cases a healthy concept of sexuality cannot be developed until these past experiences and accompanying feelings are addressed. Adolescent females who have been victims of incest will usually operate out of a shame-based orientation in future relationships, choosing destructive relationships to perpetuate their self-blame. They may continue their pattern of unresolved issues of incest by setting themselves up to be powerless and further victimized in relationships.

Chemically dependent males and females tend to present to the world a pseudomaturity to cover feelings of loss and pain in their growth and development. Although they appear to act much older than they are and often exhibit seductive behaviors, emotionally they remain unprepared to face their own sexuality issues. Their charming personalities and ability to manipulate people into believing that they "have it all together" serve as a defense mechanism to mask the anger, hurt, pain, and guilt as a result of being involved in a harmful addiction.

Tammy was eleven years old when her alcoholic father began to approach her sexually. She didn't know what to do, so she did nothing at all. She kept the situation to herself but began to dread those evenings when her mother was working nights, because she knew that her dad would get drunk and come into her room. Tammy never questioned that it wasn't her fault. She kept all the feelings of self-blame and guilt inside, along with a growing feeling of resentment toward her father. She couldn't tell her mom because it would hurt her, so she kept it to herself. Tammy began drinking at thirteen years old and had a serious alcohol problem by the time she was fifteen. It wasn't until Tammy was in treatment for her own addiction that she told her counselor about the incest.

Tammy—age 15

The resolution of sexuality issues is crucial to the adolescent's sense of self. Adolescents must be able to trust the adults in their lives to share their fears and confusion and in some cases to protect them, as with those who have been victims of incest or sexual trauma. Young people who can share their feelings and work through these painful issues begin to experience a healthy orientation toward themselves and their sexuality.

The dependent adolescent suffers in the development of his emotional and physical well-being, his spiritual life, and his sexuality. Their suffering is often more pronounced for children from alcoholic and other dysfunctional families, innocents who were forced to cope and survive under adverse circumstances. Their task in sobriety involves facing the loss not only of their chemicals, but of their very childhoods. They must recognize and acknowledge their drinking and drugging in connection with these losses if they are ever to achieve and maintain sobriety.

Relationships are affected while an adolescent is developing a harmful dependency on chemicals. As the dependency becomes more pronounced, as the addict's behavior grows more out of control, so do his relationships with family, teachers, and peers. In fact, "out of control" is the phrase often used by parents to describe their relationship with a dependent son or daughter. Communication deteriorates as the addicted adolescent breaks promises, home rules, and guidelines. Hostile, angry fights between parents and their sons or daughters create emotional distance and turmoil within the home.

Tom began using cocaine and drinking alcohol when he was fourteen years old. He began to spend more time alone in his room, refusing to go on any family outings and becoming sarcastic and cynical toward his parents whenever they would question him about where he was spending his money and his time. They began to suspect that he was involved with drugs but hoped that they were wrong. The night Tom entered an inpatient treatment center for alcoholism, he and his father had an argument that led to a physical fight. It was the impetus for the family to take action and make a decision to no longer live that way.

Tom—age 15

The relationship between parents and their addicted child often becomes one of distrust, resentment, and fear.

The adolescent becomes increasingly withdrawn and uncommunicative in relating to the adults in his life, particularly parents. The anger and hostility from the addicted teenager leaves most parents feeling angry, frustrated, and guilty for not having been "better parents."

One of the primary reasons these relationships are unbalanced and unhealthy has to do with the progression of the disease. Dependent adolescents become accustomed to living a lie through their dependency, deceiving parents about their friends and social life in order to cover up the extent of chemical usage. This dishonesty makes it extremely difficult for parents, teachers, or counselors to form a meaningful relationship with an actively using addicted young person. Healthy relationships require sharing of feelings, openness, and a willingness to negotiate when problems and difficulties arise. The adolescent involved in a harmful dependency is unable to relate to others in this manner.

"I used to lie to my parents about things that I didn't even need to lie about. It just became a habit, I guess. I always felt that if I told them what they wanted to hear, things would be better. Only, things only got worse. I was admitted to an inpatient unit for alcoholism when I was sixteen years old and wouldn't speak to my parents for the first week I was in treatment. I was so angry that they put me into a treatment center. I wasn't willing to look at myself yet. I just focused on how angry I was with them. I met with them and started to get honest about my feelings and our relationship. Today we have a neat relationship, and I can talk to them about almost anything. We still have our problems, but we always manage to work them out. I feel pretty lucky to have parents who are always there for me."

Chris—age 17

The entire family is affected when there is an actively using chemically dependent young person in the home. The disease becomes just as powerful for family members living with a young person who is harmfully involved with alcohol and drugs.

The adolescent who begins a recovery process from a chemical addiction is able to progress and experience personal growth in all areas of development. Through abstinence from all mood-altering chemicals and the necessary therapeutic interventions, recovering young people can develop the tools to live healthy, happy lives without chemicals. Those who have begun their recovery process seem to bear out this simple truth.

"I have been sober for one year and three days. I am having fun in my sobriety today, and I never thought it could be possible. Oh, I had some catching up to do at school, with my relationship with my parents and with the way that I handled my problems. But, one day at a time I worked at my problems, and things did get better. I have grown a lot, and I feel like I deserve the payoffs that I'm getting from all of my hard work. In AA we say that we 'claim progress, not perfection,' and that seems to really fit for me."

Tom—age 16

Parents can motivate a young person to accept treatment for a primary and fatal disease. The important role parents play in the dependent adolescent's recovery process cannot be overstressed. Interventions to get adolescents into treatment for their disease are usually accomplished through parents' care and concern. Their ongoing support and firm but caring insistence that things had to change was the impetus to accept treatment for many adolescents now recovering from this disease.

CHAPTER 4

Children of Alcoholics with Dependency Problems

Children of Alcoholics with drug and alcohol dependencies bring special issues with them to relationships and to their own recovery process. A high percentage of adolescents with chemical health problems come from families with a background of alcoholism and drug dependencies. Alcoholism runs in families, making Children of Alcoholics much more susceptible to the development of addictions.

Recent research and statistics indicate that nearly 70 percent of those adolescents diagnosed as chemically dependent and alcoholic have at least one parent with a drinking problem or drug addiction. Children of Alcoholics seem to possess both genetic and psychological characteristics that predispose them to developing the disease of chemical dependency.

The National Association for Children of Alcoholics Charter Statement describes these facts as they relate to Children of Alcoholics:

- An estimated twenty-eight million Americans (seven million of them under eighteen) have at least one alcoholic parent.
- Children of Alcoholics are at the highest risk of becoming alcoholic or marrying someone who becomes alcoholic.

- One of three families currently reports alcohol abuse by a family member.
- Children of Alcoholics are prone to a range of psychological difficulties, including learning disabilities, anxiety, attempted and completed suicide, eating disorders, and compulsive achieving.
- COAs often adapt to the chaos and inconsistency of an alcoholic home by developing an inability to trust, an extreme need to control, an excessive sense of responsibility, and a denial of feelings, all of which result in low self-esteem, depression, isolation, guilt, and difficulty maintaining satisfying relationships. These and other problems often persist throughout adulthood.
- More than half of all alcoholics have an alcoholic parent.
- Children of Alcoholics are frequently victims of incest, child abuse, and other forms of violence and exploitation.
- The problems of most COAs remain invisible because their coping behavior tends to be approval seeking and socially acceptable. However, a disproportionate number of those entering the juvenile justice system, courts, prisons, and mental health facilities are COAs.[1]

Some young people who have grown up watching a parent move through the progression of alcoholism will later develop their own addiction. Others may not have lived with an alcoholic parent owing to a separation or divorce. The important factors seem to be their genetic predisposition toward the disease and the fact that their lives have been touched by parental alcoholism.

Children of Alcoholics need primary prevention programs to address their needs. Millions of children who sit in American classrooms come from alcoholic or drug-dependent families. Statistics indicate that perhaps one out of every four children in any classroom is from an alcoholic family.

Only within the last several years has the impact on children growing up in alcoholic families been truly recognized. The consequences they suffer socially, emotionally, and academically are being recognized with the help of such programs as the National Elementary School Project for Children of Alcoholics, sponsored by the National Association for Children of Alcoholics in cooperation with the Center for Substance Abuse Services and the U.S. Department of Education. Titled "It's Elementary," the program provides teachers and other school personnel with the tools to identify and appropriately refer Children of Alcoholics to helping services. Programs geared to address the emotions and attitudes created by living with active alcoholism and drug addiction play an important role in arresting the generational cycle of addiction.

Alcoholism need not be present in the family for children to suffer the losses discussed in this chapter. With today's changing family structure, many children are affected by divorce, death, or in some cases the physical absence of their parents. Any family that suffers such a traumatic change goes through a period of grieving and readjustment. Some children will adjust to the changes with relatively little difficulty, while others will experience the loss much more profoundly.

Adolescents from alcoholic and other families of trauma often go unrecognized until they get into some type of trouble, facilitating a referral to the juvenile justice system, department of social services, or an alcoholism treatment setting. With rare exceptions, the programs currently in place to help small children and older adults from an alcoholic family are not yet available to adolescents. An adolescent is likely to receive help for the issues related to his alcoholic family once he has been referred to an alcoholism treatment program or a psychiatric mental health facility.

Clearly, more services are needed to identify and appropriately address the needs of the adolescent living in an alcoholic or other dysfunctional family environment *prior* to his entrance into the social service system.

Adolescents who develop dependencies on chemicals seem to view alcoholism from a personal perspective, given how they have seen their alcoholic parent function at home. Many adolescents will describe alcoholics as those who drink all day, who need alcohol to survive, who can no longer function. Although all these perceptions are true for someone in the chronic phases of alcoholism, they do not describe the actively drinking and functioning parent that many Children of Alcoholics have experienced at home.

Adolescent Children of Alcoholics may have a strong and binding relationship with their alcoholic parent, no matter how destructive that relationship appears. Loyalty to the alcoholic parent is not easily broken. Many adolescents have been raised hearing double messages from their alcoholic parent. The parent who gets drunk and then tells his son or daughter that he will "kill them" if he finds out that they are using "drugs" sends a confusing and contradictory message to the young person. The relationship with the alcoholic parent, although often confusing, continues to be a powerful source of identification and comparison for the adolescent developing an addiction to chemicals. How can the adolescent really have a problem with chemicals if his alcoholic parent has been drinking heavily for years and is still drinking?

Tammy sat in group therapy one day discussing her father's drinking. She described the violent outbursts that occurred when he drank whiskey. She didn't think of him as an alcoholic. She knew that he wouldn't let his drinking go that far. Her dad was "too smart" to be an alcoholic.

Tammy—age 15

The adolescent's definition of alcoholism and drug dependencies is based upon what he has experienced and seen in his own home. If the alcoholic parent is still functioning, the adolescent may perceive his parent as drinking too much but not acknowledge their alcoholism for what it is. Denial runs deep for any young person coming out of an alcoholic home environment; it is a survival technique used to cope in an unhealthy situation.

Family Secrets

Children of Alcoholics become experts at keeping secrets about the problems caused by alcoholism in the home. No one talks about the alcoholism or acknowledges that the problems are the result of the parent's drinking problem. Most adolescents observe their nondrinking codependent parent telling lies about the spouse's drinking, covering up for him or her at work and acting as if nothing were wrong at home. The denial is reinforced daily as the parent's disease progresses and no one discusses it.

Children of Alcoholics also become skilled at covering up and lying. They do not talk about what is really going on at home and act as if everything is all right even when it isn't. They keep the "family secret" at all costs, because to break it would mean they are being disloyal to their alcoholic parent.

Once an adolescent begins to use chemicals himself, the denial continues in relation to his own usage. Comparing his usage to that of his alcoholic parent, he comes in a close second. Many young people from alcoholic homes will deliberately use drugs other than alcohol to reinforce their decision not to become like their alcoholic parent.

Keeping the family secret becomes an unspoken expectation. Keeping secrets about the extent of their own chemical usage becomes the norm for Children of Alcoholics.

Adults Can't Be Trusted

Adolescents who have grown up in alcoholic families have experienced the disappointment that comes from trusting their alcoholic parent. They learn that adults break promises. And as more promises are broken, adolescents learn that settling for less is a way of life.

It is important to note that Children of Alcoholics exhibit the behaviors created by the disease without ever taking their first drink or drug. In denying the disease of their parent, they develop attitudes toward alcohol they are not even aware of. They have watched the disease progress in their home and have begun to accept, as normal, very abnormal behaviors. Their reference points are what they have observed and experienced.

Trusting adults is too great a risk for the adolescent who has experienced pain from trusting in the past. They learn to trust only themselves and to not need their parents. This self-sufficient exterior is a cover to prevent further confusion and sadness resulting from their parent's alcoholism.

Some adolescents have had to assume the parenting role within the home as alcoholism in the family has progressed. They may serve in this capacity to their own parents or to their younger brothers and sisters.

Cathy came into treatment for alcoholism at the age of sixteen. She had been functioning as a parent to both her parents since she was twelve years old. Her mother and father were both alcoholic and unable to provide Cathy with the nurturing and care that she needed during her childhood years. Cathy listened sympathetically to her parents' problems, trying to help all she could with running the house and meeting their needs.

She began to drink when she was fourteen years old and found relief from the pressures of being responsible for so many tasks at home. She progressed to drinking alone at home when both parents were passed out and she was taking care of the household tasks.

Cathy smiled a lot and acted as if everything were just fine. She didn't really think that her alcoholism was all that severe, despite the concerns of her school counselor and teachers. Cathy had been caught drunk at school on two occasions in her morning classes. Her disease was progressing much more quickly than it had for either of her parents. After only two years of drinking, Cathy was already experiencing uncontrollable usage of alcohol.

Cathy—age 16

Everything Is Just Fine

Most Children of Alcoholics will tell you "Everything is just fine." They have learned how to minimize their feelings well and don't have much experience at letting others know how they really feel inside. Most Children of Alcoholics feel very intensely but must shut down their feeling processes in order to function and cope with the realities of a parental drinking problem.

Children of Alcoholics become used to the mood swings created within their home environment. The only consistency they may have experienced is the fact of their parent's alcoholism. Beyond that, they cannot predict what will happen on a given evening in their home.

Children of Alcoholics swing frequently from sad to happy, depending upon the circumstances in their home environment. If a promise is made and kept by their alcoholic parent, they may shift from sad to happy and not even understand their mood swing, other than it feels good. They rarely function in the peaceful, normal range of feelings. As the disease progresses in their home environment, their moods begin to depend upon those of their alcoholic parent. If a promise is broken, they swing from happy to sad, realizing that things really haven't changed.

Their belief system is reinforced. You really can't trust adults, and it surely would be a lot easier not to have to keep going through this pain. To not feel becomes a survival technique. Shutting off intense feelings and refusing to acknowledge them becomes a much easier way to cope with the disease of alcoholism in the home. Verbalizing that "it really doesn't matter, anyway" helps; it helps to feel tough inside and to not have to feel so vulnerable all the time. Replacing intense feelings of sadness, anger, and disappointment with a new defense system also helps for a while.

Hal, a sixteen-year-old male in treatment for his own chemical dependency, looked down with tears in his eyes as he described what growing up in an alcoholic home had been like for him. At eight years old, Hal had wanted desperately to spend time with his alcoholic father. He had not realized that his father was in the acute stages of alcoholism and was unable to respond to Hal's need. That particular summer, Hal had sat by the front window waiting for his father to come home. But nine o'clock would come and Hal's father would not be home yet. Hal would go to bed disappointed and sad.

At some point that summer, Hal decided that it really didn't matter anymore if his father came home. Eight years had passed since Hal had told himself that it just didn't matter.

Today Hal is just beginning to feel how much it really did matter that his father didn't spend time with him that summer or many summers after that. Hal is the child of an alcoholic parent. What makes this truth even more difficult is that Hal is also working on the acceptance of his own disease of chemical dependency.

Hal—age 16

Many people seem somewhat surprised that a COA would turn to the same coping mechanism to approach life. Comments such as "Wouldn't they have learned watching what alcohol has done to their alcoholic parent?" become less significant once chemical dependency is understood in the context of having a "love relationship" with chemicals.

Children of Alcoholics approach their usage with the strong belief that they intend to have a different experience. But an amazing thing happens for most COAs. They feel good when they take a drink or smoke a joint. They can forget about the pain, laugh with friends, feel more confident, and even express feelings to others. They have just accomplished a mood swing with the ingestion of a chemical, and they *feel good*. This new experience may cause feelings of guilt and confusion in the young person, but the temporary good feelings certainly outweigh guilt. Guilt and confusion are familiar feelings to Children of Alcoholics. Adolescent Children of Alcoholics usually feel guilty and responsible for their parent's drinking whether or not they have received parental messages to this effect. If only they did better in school or didn't fight so much with their brothers and sisters, maybe their alcoholic parent wouldn't drink so much.

Good feelings can be experienced with chemicals. Painful feelings can be changed with chemicals. For the COA that first experience with chemicals is usually a positive experience. They're beginning to feel complete, accepted by their peers, and, most important, feeling good.

Jackie, referred to the inpatient unit for a serious chemical dependency problem, had been labeled incorrigible owing to her frequent runaway episodes and truancy from school. She had been seen by two psychiatrists during the past year and had been placed on home detention through the juvenile courts for the past six months. Despite these interventions, Jackie had continued to use alcohol and other chemicals. Teenage Jackie seemed more like a twenty-year-old as she discussed her home life and her parent's alcoholism. She had been taking care of "the boys" during the past four years as her father's alcoholism had worsened. Her mother often went with her father to the bars at night to make sure that he didn't drink too much and to get him home safely. Jackie and her two younger brothers were left on their own the evenings her parents were at the bar, and Jackie had assumed more and more responsibility for her brothers.

Jackie's father went through alcoholism treatment when she was fourteen years old, and shortly after that, Jackie began to drink and use marijuana. She began to drink with her friends, now free of the responsibilities of caring for her younger brothers. She described her first drinking episode as "great." She was able to laugh and have a good time. She began drinking alone when her parents were gone at night to AA and Al-Anon meetings. She didn't think she would have a problem handling her alcohol.

Jackie was in the acute stages of alcoholism when her parents admitted her for treatment. Quitting alcohol was not easy for Jackie because she missed the "good feeling." She began to cry as she said, "I never wanted to be an alcoholic like my father. I really like alcohol, and this just isn't fair. I still think that I can drink once in a while, and I just may when I get out of this place."

Jackie had not yet realized that she was one of the lucky young people who was diagnosed properly and treated for a disease that only gets worse as long as the drinking continues.

Jackie—age 16

Young people who begin to use alcohol and other chemicals may find that altering feelings this way works—for a while. They have little awareness that their own disease will progress much more rapidly when they use more than one chemical at a time. They are even less aware of the hormonal changes due to their physical growth and the acceleration of their disease. Although using drugs and alcohol works for a while, the consequences of their disease become more severe as their usage intensifies. Children of Alcoholics eventually discover that their own alcoholism and chemical dependency problems are exactly what they have been trying to escape from in their own home environment.

Roles Assumed in Alcoholic Homes by Children

Extensive work has been done in the alcoholism field defining the roles Children of Alcoholics assume in the home to cope with the inconsistency and pain caused by parental alcoholism. Adolescents continue with these roles into their young adulthood and do not realize that they no longer work for them in productive ways.

Scapegoat
The scapegoat role is usually assumed by adolescents who are angry and sad about parental alcoholism and choose to act out those feelings. They will take negative attention over no attention at all. This role is often entered into by young people who are hostile and defiant toward their alcoholic parent and choose to get their needs met through their peer group rather than their family. They become the "black sheep" of the family and are often compared with their alcoholic parent by such comments as "You know, you are going to be just like your father." Adolescents playing out the scapegoat role may begin using chemicals at an early age, be involved in the legal system at an early age, have unplanned pregnancies, run away from home, or be ex-

pelled from school for truancy, failing grades, or repeated offenses of drunken behavior in classes.

Family Hero

This role is often assumed by the adolescent who wants to achieve success outside his family to compensate for the feelings of inadequacy so familiar to him. He represents self-worth to the family through such comments as "Isn't it amazing how well Greg does despite all of his family's problems?" The family hero is the high achiever, getting good grades, excelling in sports, and having a lot of friends and interests outside his family. Family heroes are invested in looking good and presenting themselves as "together" to the outside world. They have chosen to detach from the family alcoholism by having their needs for acceptance met outside the home. They are very responsible, both at home and at school. They are dependable and well organized in an attempt to cope with the chaotic atmosphere of their alcoholic home.

Lost Child

The adolescent who assumes the lost child role in the family retreats into himself to cope with the frustrations of growing up in an alcoholic home. He is usually very quiet and withdrawn and feels unimportant within the family structure. He may have few friends, be a follower, and have trouble making decisions. He would rather retreat into himself than cope with the alcoholism in his home. The quiet, lonely, lost child can remain almost invisible, which is exactly the way he wants it.

Family Mascot

The mascot assumes the role of comic relief within the alcoholic home. This is the adolescent child who covers his fear by being funny, and he thereby receives a lot of attention for his humor, both at school and at home. He may be a frustrating adolescent to work with or spend time with, as he has difficulty sitting still and has a short attention span. He presents a very immature exterior to the world and often looks as if he needs protection. His compulsive clowning around usually gets him into trouble at school but is often a welcome relief within the serious alcoholic home atmosphere.

All these roles that Children of Alcoholics assume are coping mechanisms as they adjust to the ever-changing environment of their alcoholic homes. These roles serve as a means to handle the confusion and sadness they experience in their families.

Adolescents entering treatment for their own chemical dependency problems are skilled at codependency behaviors as well. They know how to enable their peers by not making them responsible for their mistakes. They have watched the entire process of alcoholism unfold at home and have learned well. Dependent adolescents have been enabling their alcoholic parent for years by keeping the "family secret." They simply do not have the resources or the reference points of healthier styles of relating or of taking care of themselves.

It is extremely important to initiate a therapeutic relationship with such adolescents. The relationships they form with their teachers and those in the helping professions will have an impact on them. It is important for them to learn to respond to the roles that they have assumed in their alcoholic home, even if the role no longer works for them or is necessary in their new environment in a treatment setting.

Scapegoat

If you are working with a young person who displays the acting-out behaviors of the scapegoat, acknowledge that his role is a protective device and that most of his defiance is based in fear. Underneath the "tough guy" image that he portrays is usually a scared and vulnerable young person who is very interested in not letting anyone know he is afraid of what has happened in his alcoholic family and what has happened to him through the progression of his own alcoholism and drug dependency.

Don't:

- allow them to hook you into power struggles.
- focus too much on their negative behavior. (They are used to adults reacting to their negative behavior.)
- take their defiance too seriously.
- allow them to make threats or intimidate others by swearing.
- take their "tough guy" image too seriously.

Do:

- give them clear and consistent expectations for their behavior.
- focus on their feelings underneath the behavior.
- provide them with ways to express their anger in constructive ways through physical activity, writing, talking, and so forth.
- help them to see that they have strengths, and focus on these strengths.
- make them leaders in a positive way through positive feedback on their leadership skills.

- believe that they can change through consistent, honest feedback on their destructive behaviors.
- love them until they can learn to love themselves.

Family Hero
Family heroes relate well to adults and display a pseudomaturity to cover up their feelings of inadequacy and poor self-esteem. They will tell you whatever you want to hear and are skilled at people pleasing and charming others. They look to externals for their good feelings, to things such as sports and academics. They usually have missed important parts of their childhood, having had to be responsible for everything and everyone other than their own needs.

Don't:

- let them continually talk about things outside themselves such as sports, grades, friends.
- let them talk in nonfeeling terms about themselves. (change "I think" statements to "I feel" statements.)
- let them isolate themselves from others through their "better than" attitude.
- allow them to give feedback to others without including themselves and their own issues in that feedback.
- expect them to give up their image too soon.

Do:

- help them to talk about their fears.
- teach them how to focus on themselves and their own issues and feelings.
- help them to learn from their mistakes, not beat themselves up for those mistakes.
- help them learn how to stroke themselves for the pos-

itive and real accomplishments they have made internally.

- encourage them to be their own age.

Lost Child

The adolescent who has assumed the lost child role in the family will often maintain that role in peer group and social settings. He will need daily and realistic goals to bolster his self-esteem and to feel a sense of accomplishment. Make your expectations clear to the adolescent in the role of the lost child and do not expect his personality to change dramatically.

Don't:

- expect them to volunteer, particularly in a group setting.
- ignore them or allow them to remain "invisible."
- allow the group to tease or make fun of them and their quietness.
- allow them to tell you only what it is they think you want to hear.

Do:

- ask their opinion as often as possible.
- help them to build their assertiveness skills.
- explore feelings, particularly about their self-image.
- find out what interests them and encourage them to share about it.
- help them to communicate their feelings through journals, poetry, collages, or creative writing.
- give them positive feedback and encouragement when you see them trying on new behaviors.

Family Mascot

If you are working with the child who has assumed the role of the mascot, his presentation may be immature and he may display a rather naïve attitude toward life. Although he may be quite humorous initially, there is an irritating quality that will drive his peers away as he continues to use humor inappropriately and, sometimes, destructively.

Don't:

- accept their excuses for their inappropriate humor or feel sorry for them.
- let them be "mascoted" in group by older, more mature adolescents.
- allow them to negate their positive qualities.
- expect them to know how to be patient or to calm themselves down when they are extremely active.

Do:

- help them to change their mistaken ideas about themselves and their need to be the center of attention.
- give them outlets to get plenty of exercise.
- teach them to calm themselves down and to tire themselves out, if necessary.
- monitor their foods, especially the amount of sweets they eat.
- individualize their treatment plan.
- be careful in your use of touch with them (help them to stay calm).

It is important to acknowledge that the roles that adolescents have assumed in coping within an alcoholic home environment have served a purpose for them, sometimes from a very early age. Some adolescents may have switched roles several times within the family, as older brothers and sisters leave home or the family dynamics change. It is important to work with adolescents to show them that these roles are no longer productive and, more important, have been used to mask painful feelings that they hold about themselves and their alcoholic home; this becomes the key in providing them with healthy alternatives for change.

Many adolescents who have assumed various roles within the family will move into the scapegoat role once an addiction to chemicals takes precedence. As their chemicals become paramount, they will further alienate themselves from the very people they want desperately to connect with emotionally, especially family members and parents. And they will become further out of touch with the many feelings they hold about themselves and their alcoholic home environment.

Children of Alcoholics begin using chemicals to meet basic needs of acceptance, to medicate their feelings, to cope with an unhealthy living environment, or to bolster their poor self-esteem. Medicating feelings works for a while for the dependent adolescent. They have little awareness that their own disease will progress much more rapidly because they are using more than one chemical at a time to experience a mood swing. They are even less aware that their disease will accelerate owing to the physiological changes of adolescence. And they honestly believe that their experience with alcohol and other chemicals will be much different from that of their alcoholic parent.

Feelings?

Expressing feelings may be a terrifying experience for Children of Alcoholics, newly sober themselves. COAs can often be easily identified in a group setting of other adolescents. They will put enormous amounts of energy and control into not letting anyone see the pain, confusion, and sadness that they have been medicating with their chemicals. Their eyes may fill up with tears, but not one tear will spill over. Acknowledge their sadness. The tears will come in time.

It is important to remember that adolescent Children of Alcoholics are being asked to express feelings they may not even know how to identify. They may have no reference point from which to begin. Many of these young people have not seen feelings expressed in their home, at least not in a constructive manner. This whole business of expressing feelings is new and scary, and they may not know where to begin.

Expressing feelings may carry with it old, familiar defense patterns like running from the situation, withdrawing or isolating themselves, or attempting to change the focus from themselves. Expressing feelings may also trigger acting-out behavior that has become a comfortable yet self-defeating life-style. As emotions begin to surface, the chemical-free adolescent may experience unidentifiable feelings of confusion, fear, and anxiety. The young person needs to know that he is in a safe environment and that his feelings of confusion are all right, even expected.

Expressing feelings is a learning experience for the adolescent child of an alcoholic parent. He needs to discover that underneath his anger toward his alcoholic parent is hurt and pain, that his feelings will not destroy him, that expressing feelings honestly is necessary for his own sobriety and recovery. He needs to be taught how ignoring his feelings and stuffing them inside has hampered his emotional health, and that he does deserve better. He needs to be acknowledged and affirmed for his feelings. He needs to learn that he has a choice. He can succeed and learn how to feel good about himself.

Julie, shy and quiet, never said too much in group, and when she did speak, her face became red and she looked at the floor. Julie slowly began risking by reaching out to the new adolescent patients who came into the treatment unit. There was a sensitive caring about Julie that the newer patients responded to positively.

As her leadership skills emerged, Julie began to confront other adolescent patients when they displayed negative behaviors that interfered with their getting well. Julie was quietly effective in maintaining a positive environment on the unit.

At Friday's group meeting, the peer and staff members tallied their ratings of each patient for cooperativeness on the unit, helpfulness toward others, and display of a positive program of recovery. Julie had the highest rating on the unit and was handed the top achievement trophy, to be kept in her room the entire week.

At 11:30 P.M. that night, the night staff member opened the door to Julie's room to check on her. She was sound asleep and the trophy she was holding was on the pillow next to her head. Julie had experienced her first taste of success.

Julie—age 15

Learning to express feelings and to affirm oneself is a brand-new task for dependent Children of Alcoholics.

Learning to identify and express feelings can best be facilitated by providing tangible, visible tools to help the young person in the process.

A feelings chart, a journal, the use of "I feel" statements to identify feelings, are all helpful tools to assist adolescents in recovery. The most important tool the therapist can use in the learning process is himself. Touching, caring, helping COAs refocus on their feelings, are crucial to their development and to their recovery process. Talking about emotions as simple as happiness, sadness, anger, fear, and shame can assist in helping the adolescent to identify his feelings. Teaching adolescent Children of Alcoholics that they will be affirmed for who they are behind their mask of "toughness" is crucial to addressing their special issues.

To sit across from a young recovering adolescent and have him look you in the eyes and say "I feel scared and kind of vulnerable when I think about going home" is real progress. Acknowledge the progress. They are learning cognitively to express feelings, even though they may not yet share all the confusing new emotions that they are experiencing in their sobriety.

Adolescents will test and push for you to set limits for them despite complaining about rules. Most dependent adolescents will thrive on the consistency in a structured group setting or in an environment where therapy is taking place. They become accustomed to adults responding to their behavior, setting limits, and making them responsible for their actions and behaviors. The behavior that they employ may be self-defeating, but they are slowly learning that they make choices every day, choices that are indicated by their actions and how they respond to the people, places, and things in their environment.

Adolescents who begin their own recovery process of

sobriety are also dealing with family issues of recovery. They have issues of trust, expression of feelings, and losses related to the emotional absence of their alcoholic parent during their formative years. But they have an early start on the choices they can make about their own lives.

It is important for the adolescent in recovery to face issues of growing up in an alcoholic family. Unless adequately addressed in the context of a treatment program, these issues may cause a relapse into alcohol and other drug use. Undoubtedly the adolescent child did a fair amount of drinking and drugging to cope with the pain of being raised in an alcoholic family. This family may include adults who are still actively drinking and using chemicals, either parents or older siblings. Such an environment impacts on the disease—their family's and their own. Failure to deal with family issues of usage will sabotage their recovery. They will most likely feel betrayed by the lack of support for their continued sobriety. Adolescents must achieve autonomy in their sobriety, autonomy from past using friends, new using acquaintances, and, in some cases, family members who are still active in their alcoholism or drug addiction.

Children of Alcoholics who are recovering from their own dependency on chemicals have learned the hard way. They have many experiences ahead of them in which they may try to use their old styles of coping and solving problems. They may remain chemical free in recovery or they may relapse and begin using chemicals again. One thing is certain, however: They have had a "taste of freedom" and a different perspective from which to approach their life. A seed has been planted that can never be displaced . . . a seed of hope.

Tobie, a fourteen-year-old in treatment for her own alcoholism, sat in group one afternoon explaining the picture she had drawn in education earlier that morning. Her picture was a blue sky, green grass, and a red sun peeking up over the horizon. She looked calm and serene as she discussed the picture that she had drawn. It looked insignificant, she stated, compared to the colorful and bright drawings of her peers, but, she continued, it represented many feelings for her, new feelings that she never knew she could feel. She no longer had an empty spot inside of her that she needed to fill with alcohol and other chemicals. She felt peaceful and hopeful inside and liked her new sobriety. She went on to state that this was the longest time she had ever gone without alcohol and drugs since she started using two years ago. She looked up from her drawing and smiled. "Maybe there really is hope on the horizon for me," she said.

Tobie—age 14

CHAPTER 5

Enabling the Adolescent

To "enable" can best be defined as assisting a person in continuing a nonproductive and often destructive behavior. Enabling usually occurs with a lack of knowledge, specifically about the diseases of alcoholism and chemical dependencies in adolescents. Enabling is usually entered into with good intentions and the desire to be helpful to the young person who is experiencing difficulties. Most parents will enable their son or daughter for the simple reason that they love their children and want to protect them from hurt and pain. It is a fine line for most parents between love and enabling.

Not understanding the disease progression of dependency, many parents become involved in the enabling process, unaware of the consequences that both they and the dependent adolescent are suffering as a result of this codependency behavior.

Parents and other family members become involved in their own disease progression and become emotionally unhealthy while living with a drug-dependent son or daughter. Their time, energy, and thought processes become focused on the dependent young person and his behavior. They may begin to police their son or daughter to ensure that no chemicals are being used. Parents may become "junior detectives" in their own homes, looking for empty bottles and other paraphernalia indicating chemical use. As the adolescent continues through his disease progression, so do family members.

Many parents may become involved in a pattern of enabling because of their own denial of the disease of dependency.

Denial

Denial is a protective device, a defense to protect oneself from painful truths. Denial is a characteristic common to chemically dependent families. Parents will look to other problems as the reason for the adolescent's continuing difficulties. Other problems can always be rationalized as the issue for the behavior the dependent adolescent is displaying.

"Tom is a good boy. I think that he's having a difficult time adjusting to high school. I knew it would be harder for him than the junior high school that he attended last year. His grades have dropped dramatically this year. I wish that I could put him in a different school. Maybe things would improve if I could just get him away from the group of friends that he's been hanging around with at the high school."

Todd
Parent

Geographical cures, including changing neighborhoods and schools in an effort to solve the problem, are common to parents prior to their understanding of the disease progression of dependency. Many parents desperately want the problem to be something other than a chemical addiction. Some parents may be embarrassed that they have a son or daughter with a chemical addiction. They may remain in denial of their child's growing dependency on chemicals.

The son or daughter who is addicted to alcohol and other drugs is often seen as a living accusation, a warped product of the mother and father's parenting skills. In many cases, a false sense of pride keeps families from seeking help to address the problem, forcing them to struggle on a daily basis with the destructive behavior of their drug-dependent child.

Denial of chemical dependencies in adolescents is not found just in the family. School systems may participate in their own denial of the problem. Parents complaining of the drug problem at school may be viewed by the school administration as overreacting. School personnel may point to the "burnouts" as the problem, in suggesting such "troublemakers" be removed from school. Or they may maintain that their school does not have a serious drug or alcohol problem, at least not serious enough to become alarmed about. Attitudes of denial and blame only keep school systems from addressing the real problem—adolescent chemical health problems—found in the majority of school systems across the United States.

Parents blaming school systems and school systems blaming the helping professionals for not "correcting" the adolescents keeps all those concerned involved in the problem. Some communities have taken a much stronger stand on the chemical health problem. Concerned parents, police, judges, schools, and youth agencies have adopted the philosophy that the chemical health problem is destroying many young people in their own community. They have chosen to do something about it. Some of these communities are forming special task forces to meet and provide solutions to the problems. Others are taking action through the media, organizing support groups to provide parents with education about adolescent drug dependencies, and de-

manding community services to address the problem.
These communities have moved out of the problem and
into the solution.

Schools and community members have worked together to design and implement student assistance programs much like the employee assistance programs that
intervene on addictions and other related problems with
adults. These school-based programs are now operating
in some elementary, junior high, and high schools nationally. They provide education, prevention, and intervention and referral services for students who have been
affected by alcoholism and related problems. Most important, many of these programs offer a nonpunitive approach to addressing chemical addictions with students.
Student assistance programs, usually run by skilled professionals, also offer support to those high-risk children
affected by family alcoholism and other traumas such as
divorce, death, or illness.

Working in conjunction with these programs, many
school administrations have developed new policies
meant to create "drug-free schools"; school personnel
are provided with a working body of knowledge and the
policies to follow should an adolescent be caught with
alcohol or other drugs in school. As opposed to kicking
him out of school for a first offense, a policy that was
adhered to by many school boards at one time, student
assistance programs and drug-free schools policies allow a student to receive an assessment, support, and a
proper referral for help. In this way, schools and communities can work together to help solve the alcohol
and drug problems of their young people.

Communities that choose to confront the problem
must address an issue that brings the problem even
closer to home: their own use of alcohol and other
mood-altering chemicals. In order to move away from

enabling the adolescent and to become aware of the role that their behavior is playing in perpetuating the problem, parents, teachers, and counselors must explore their own usage and make changes, if necessary.

Over 50 percent of all children born to alcoholic or drug-dependent parents will go on to develop a chemical addiction problem. With numbers as high as these, all parents who drink need to focus energy and time on the impact of their drinking on their children, genetically, environmentally, and psychologically. Kids are particularly adept at noticing an adult's message of "Do as I say, not as I do!"

Likewise, adults involved in helping young people, including school personnel and mental health professionals, are encouraged to assess their own usage in order to deal accurately with teenage addiction. The adult professional's comfort level in dealing with alcoholism and other drug-related problems will have a direct impact on his effectiveness in intervening with the adolescent's addiction.

Many adults who oppose a young person's use of illegal drugs such as cocaine, crack, marijuana, and designer drugs see no real harm in drinking alcohol themselves. This discrepancy is one that all communities need to focus on as they formulate the "war on drugs."

Covering Up

Covering up the messes that the dependent adolescent gets himself into as a result of his ongoing usage is a characteristic of enabling. As long as someone, whether a parent, teacher, or mental health professional, will cover up for him, he can remain irresponsible. He will not have to suffer the consequences of his using behavior. Each time the significant adult covers up or lies for him, he learns that he can manipulate his way out of his messes, even if it means being dishonest. For a drug-dependent adolescent, the means justify the end. Being untruthful becomes second nature.

Parents become accustomed to covering up their son's or daughter's messes with the legal system and at school. Unaware that this enabling behavior is doing more harm than good, they continue in a vicious cycle, and things only worsen at home. Often, to balance the angry outbursts that are occurring with increasing frequency at home, one parent may cover up for his son or daughter to a greater degree than the other parent.

"It was two A.M., and Bruce was not home yet. He was supposed to be home by midnight, but he was late again. I couldn't sleep, even though his father had been asleep for some time. I was relieved that his father was asleep because there have been some pretty angry scenes at our house when Bruce has come home drunk. Anyway, I was looking out the window when I heard a car pull up, and I saw Bruce get out. He was stumbling and laughing as the car pulled away. He stood out in the front yard and didn't even seem to know which house was his. As I watched him trying to walk up the front steps, I almost cried. I didn't tell his father about it. Bruce's father is so angry with him these days that I get scared. I just don't want any more big scenes."

Doris
Parent

Professional enablers, unaware of the disease of dependency in the adolescent that they are treating, may continue to provide emotional support and guidance to the young person who is having a "tough" time at home and at school. The counseling relationship, defined as helping someone to help himself, takes on an added dynamic when working with a chemically dependent adolescent. The charming and manipulative behaviors of dependent adolescents are used to engage adults away from the real issue—chemical dependency. Even professionals skilled in adolescent development and counseling may become unknowingly involved in the disease process of a drug-dependent adolescent.

"Sue has been involved in counseling with me for the past nine months. Her mother is an alcoholic. Things get very unhealthy at home for Sue. It wasn't until she was suspended for possession of marijuana twice during the last several months that I was alerted to her drug problem. Granted, she has a lot of other problems, but I didn't see her drug problem as a key issue. I guess that explains why Sue never makes much progress in therapy with me and why things continue to worsen at home for her."

Marla
Youth Counselor

Many adolescents who enter a counseling situation have a variety of issues, including family problems, that need to be explored and resolved. Although these problems cannot be negated, they may cloud the primary issue—the adolescent's drug or alcohol addiction. The other problems will continue and probably worsen until the drug-dependent young person is treated for the disease.

Awareness of the symptoms and behaviors associated with drug dependencies in young people becomes crucial for parents, teachers, and counselors emotionally involved with the young person. Continuing to enable his usage only keeps him sick and prevents him from receiving the help that is imperative to treating the disease.

Fixing the Trouble

Chemically dependent families become accustomed to crises and problems. For parents of addicted teenagers, fixing the trouble caused by suspensions from school, paying for drunk-driving tickets, and paying for car accidents and legal costs becomes a way of life. Intervening in this way may appear to be the solution, but in the end it only allows the adolescent to avoid experiencing the painful consequences of his disease.

> *"We bailed Terry out of jail two weeks ago when he was picked up for speeding and drunk driving. It was three in the morning, and we had to go to work the next day. We got up and went to the police station anyway. When we walked in to pick Terry up, she looked scared and embarrassed. She began to cry and promised us that she was going to quit drinking and that she had learned her lesson this time.*
>
> *Two weeks later she came home drunk again. We are sick about it. Her promises just don't mean anything anymore. This is hard for us because Terry used to be so trustworthy."*
>
> *Karen*
> *Parent*

The adolescent in trouble with his addiction and the consequences caused by his chemical usage will promise anything. Promises made during a crisis usually carry little weight—not that the adolescent does not fully intend to keep his promise *at the time*. In most cases the young person honestly believes that this will be the last time he will get into trouble with his usage. Next time he will be more careful. Or maybe he really believes he is going to quit using alcohol and other chemicals. The compulsion to use despite harmful consequences is one of the key characteristics of the disease. The adolescent addict has not yet realized that he is no longer in control. Drugs and alcohol are now in control of his life. Parents enabling the adolescent by bailing him out of his messes have usually not yet realized that they are dealing with a powerful disease, not just isolated incidences of poor judgment on the part of a son or daughter.

Lowering Expectations

Parents attempting to cope with a drug-dependent son or daughter commonly lower their expectations. It may seem to be much easier than hassling with the adolescent to come home at a set time, clean his room, finish his school assignment, or attend family functions. Yet giving in to the adolescent in this fashion accomplishes nothing other than to reinforce his irresponsibility.

"Tim never comes home on time, and I know that he is high almost every time that he does come home. I finally just gave up. I extended his curfew because of the fights that we used to have about it, and besides, he never came home at the set time anyway. He's always saying he wants to move out or live in a foster home, but I tell him that it wouldn't be any different there. I just don't know what else to do. I get so tired of fighting with him. It worries me that his younger siblings see him coming and going pretty much as he pleases. They will probably get the idea that they don't have to follow our house rules, either."

Ted
Parent

Lowering expectations does not help to address the issue in a chemically dependent family. Many families resort to this technique of parenting when they have exhausted all other possibilities. But things continue to worsen.

As with the other enabling behaviors, lowering expectations is not restricted to the dependent adolescent's family. Lack of knowledge of the disease on the part of teachers and school personnel may cause them, too, to lower their expectations, particularly if a nonconforming relationship was present with the teenager prior to his chemical usage.

"Joe has been in my drafting class this past year, and I've worked really hard with him. He's a neat kid, but he's had a rough year. I guess I've tried to make things a little bit easier for him. Lately he's been sleeping in my class during the instruction segment of the course. He's pulling a D in class right now, and the semester is almost over. I'll have to flunk him unless he turns in his project for a grade. He just doesn't seem to care anymore. He may be deeper into drugs than I thought he was."

Steve
Drafting teacher

Blaming the Adolescent

Some parents may blame their son or daughter for their behavior, unaware of their disease. Parents operating without the knowledge necessary to change their behavior toward a dependent child may believe that that child would quit using harmful chemicals if he only loved his parents more, respected them more, or was simply more disciplined. If the teenager really loved his parents, he would straighten up and follow the rules and guidelines set down and quit causing all this trouble.

"I don't know Sandy anymore. She has caused us more grief and trouble than any of our other kids. She comes and goes as she pleases, and we're always getting calls from school that she is in trouble again or she's skipping classes. The last time we got a call from school, the principal told us that she is being suspended for possession of marijuana. She has no respect for authority, for school, or for us. She just isn't worth all this trouble. We never had this with our other kids. As far as I'm concerned, she can do what she wants to do from now on. She doesn't show us any respect, and I don't intend to show her any respect, either."

Larry
Parent

Blaming the adolescent for the behavior caused by his disease accomplishes nothing. The adolescent involved in a harmful dependency on alcohol and other drugs will continue to display irresponsible behavior until he receives intervention in the disease process and abstains from all mood-altering chemicals in conjunction with treatment.

Going to Any Lengths

Some parents become obsessed with the behavior of their drug-dependent son or daughter and become committed to ensuring that he or she will not use alcohol or other chemicals. The parent may follow the adolescent to school, pick up his child from school, and monitor each and every activity to meet the goal that he has set for his son or daughter. It is an impossible goal to reach. Chemically dependent adolescents will use chemicals no matter what restrictions are placed on them not to use them. It is the nature of the disease. Where there is a will, there is a way.

John described his response to the uncontrollable behavior of his daughter, Chris, calmly and without much emotion. Apparently Chris had begun to come and go from home as she pleased. She often came home either drunk or stoned, and her father was becoming increasingly distressed about her. John grounded Chris from all outside activities, and, although his disciplinary action worked initially, Chris soon began to leave the house without her father's permission. John was furious and frustrated with Chris's lack of respect for home rules and guidelines. He could no longer control his own daughter.

Finally John told Chris that she was grounded and could not go out that evening. Angry words and an argument followed, with Chris swearing at her father and running upstairs to lock herself in her room. John was so angry that he was frightened, but he told himself that he had to maintain control of the situation and, more important, of Chris. He ran to the basement and grabbed his hammer and nails. If he had to nail her bedroom door shut to make sure that she didn't leave that night, then that's what he would do. John began to feel secure and relieved knowing that Chris would be home that night and that he wouldn't have to lie awake worrying about her coming home drunk or stoned, or not at all. He waited a few minutes and then picked up the hammer and nails and nailed his daughter's door shut. He continued to talk to Chris through the door, calming himself at the same time. He explained why he was protecting her and that he cared only about her safety.

An hour or so later John picked up his hammer and pulled the nails out of his daughter's bedroom door. He would sit and talk with her, and they would get things straightened out between them. He opened the door, and Chris was gone. The bedroom window was open; the curtain was blowing in the breeze. John sat down and began to cry. Chris was gone again, and he knew that he wouldn't sleep again that night.

John
Parent

Parents and other adults who become emotionally involved with the dependent adolescent do not want to believe that this young person who means a great deal to them is out of control with a drug problem. They may be able to see what is happening to their son or daughter but are unaware of what is happening to themselves. Denial of the real problem and repressing their own painful emotions related to the behavior of the dependent adolescent moves them into a cycle of codependency and, in some cases, blame toward the young person and the mistaken belief that "if my child only loved me more, he wouldn't treat me like this."

Blaming the adolescent and giving up on him becomes a negative focus for the entire family. The parent who honestly believes that his child would change if he only had more respect for his parents or loved them more is setting himself up for continued pain. The dependent adolescent does not respect authority, and as he progresses in his drug dependency, he no longer respects himself. Blaming an adolescent for his addiction will only make the living environment an unhealthy place and decrease the chances that the young person will seek help for his chemical problem.

Family members, especially parents, will need to accept the seriousness of chemical dependency and the impact that the disease has had on them and the entire family unit. By doing so, they take the focus off the destructive behavior of the addicted child and place it where they have control—on their responses to their child's behavior.

Most parents have been preoccupied with their child's behavior and have tried unsuccessfully to control that child's usage. This preoccupation has directly affected their emotional and physical health, often resulting in worry, anger, inability to sleep, and guilt for not being "better parents."

The chemical dependency has probably also affected their marriage and social life, as the parents have tried to adjust to the ongoing crises created when a child of theirs becomes harmfully involved with chemicals. These crises have caused ongoing conflict within the family, often resulting in increased arguments with their spouse (usually related directly to the handling of their chemically dependent child). Many parents no longer entertain guests in their home or take weekend vacations since they do not want to be too far from the phone in case of a crisis. Many parents are simply feeling too guilty and ashamed to face their friends or to participate in activities they once enjoyed. These consequences must be faced if parents and other family members truly want to change their relationship with their chemically addicted son or daughter and regain their emotional and physical health.

The Solution

Parents, teachers, and counselors of adolescents involved in a harmful chemical dependency need to become aware of the disease and the possibility that their child, student, or client may be involved. As with any other disease, those concerned with the afflicted adolescent need to obtain as much information as they can on the diseases of alcoholism and chemical dependencies. The destructive and self-defeating behavior of the adolescent is really only a symptom of the problem; the core issue must be addressed.

Although teachers and professional counselors cope with the adolescent experiencing chemical health problems, the young person's parents and family members are usually the most seriously affected. Getting out of the problem and into the solution may take time, energy, and a commitment to change. Most families are willing to make that commitment once they have a clear understanding of the disease and their part in the healing process.

Parents of drug-dependent adolescents need to understand that they have choices. They need to explore their choices and seek all the support they can, to better address a drug or alcohol problem in their home. They do not have to suffer alone. Many parents have had to deal with the painful acknowledgment that their son or daughter is chemically involved.

Parents of chemically involved adolescents are not obliged to

• cover up and lie for their drug-dependent son or daughter's behavior.

- make excuses to family, friends, and neighbors about their child's behavior.
- allow their drug-dependent son or daughter to keep alcohol and other chemicals in the home because it is "their right."
- become an active participant in verbal or physical abuse from a son or daughter.
- allow their child to keep drug paraphernalia in their home, including pipes, rolling papers for marijuana, and so forth.
- bail their son or daughter out of the messes that they get themselves into as a result of their addiction.
- give their son or daughter the family car when they know that their child will be drinking and driving.
- act as if everything is all right at home even if it isn't.
- try to handle the problem on their own because they are embarrassed by "what other people will think."[1]

Helping the dependent adolescent to accept responsibility for "owning" his addiction is a necessary step to breaking through the denial, arresting the adolescent's manipulation of those involved with him emotionally, and altering the young addict's self-deceptive attitude that he has no problem with alcohol or other chemicals. Suffering consequences and losses as a result of his continued chemical usage may mobilize the adolescent toward treatment.

Creating consequences is also required for the adolescent to begin experiencing the pain that his addiction is causing in his life. This is often a turning point in acceptance of the disease. The adolescent may become tired of being "sick and tired," a phrase often heard in Alcoholics Anonymous. Parents may serve as a catalyst for the adolescent in this: their refusal to cover up, fix the problem, bail their child out of his messes, or lower their expectations. Parents can be the impetus needed for the dependent young person to accept treatment for his disease.

Parents need to remember that each time they enable their son or daughter, they are robbing their child of the growth necessary to accept his primary, progressive, and fatal disease.

CHAPTER 6

Learning the Hard Way—
The Adolescent in Recovery

Adolescents who become dependent on alcohol and other mood-altering chemicals have experienced life from a much different perspective from that of young people who do not develop such harmful dependencies. Dependent young people operate out of the mistaken belief that they are infallible and that bad things happen to other people but not to them. They may honestly believe that they do not have a chemical abuse problem and that they can quit using anytime they choose. Denial runs deep for dependent young people and is part of the disease progression.

Certain themes seem to be present in all adolescents who become involved in a harmful dependency. Although each individual will encounter different experiences in the development of his disease, every drug-dependent adolescent has constructed various defense systems to protect himself from an honest appraisal of the situation and from the fear of giving up an ongoing relationship with chemicals.

Dependent adolescents become excellent manipulators as their disease progresses. They learn to live a lie through their use of chemicals, all the time acting as if they do not have a problem with drugs. Dependent adolescents have the ability to switch the focus from their own negative behaviors by blaming other places, things, and people, particularly significant others, for their difficulties. Alibis, excuses, and lies are common in the adolescent's explanation of how he got involved in difficulties and problems. Blaming others becomes a way of life for the chemically dependent adolescent. Parents seem to be the likeliest candidates for blame placing. If the parent would just change, the adolescent would not have to drink so much or get high so often.

Parents are blamed for being too strict, too protective, or too untrusting or for not understanding the young person at all. Parents, especially if they feel insecure about their parenting skills, may accept this blame as the truth. Questioning their skills as a parent, they may avoid further confrontations with the young person or retaliate by placing the blame back on the adolescent. Both these patterns of communication become unhealthy for both parties. Although parents may assume the enabling role in the family disease, their parenting is not the sole reason for the adolescent's chemical usage. Enabling parents are part of the problem, not its cause.

Dependent adolescents can appear very "together" and at the same time unapproachable. Many chemically involved young people present themselves as "having it all together," even if they feel as though they are falling apart inside. They manage to create a certain emotional distance that can instill doubt in the most secure adult. This doubt is created by the adolescent's conflicting presentation of himself. Even though tangible signs of chemical abuse may be present, adults may assume that the young person is doing all right, given his continued untruths and verbalization that all is fine. Dependent adolescents can make themselves look good in the most questionable situations. Their actions always speak louder than their words. Adults involved on an emotional level with a dependent adolescent need continually to remind themselves of this simple truth.

The image of "having it all together" fits with the dependent adolescent's minimization of truth and reality, particularly in relation to his chemical usage. He will tell you whatever it is he thinks you want to hear. He will tell you that he hasn't gotten high for over a month, that the alcohol in his possession belongs to his friends, that the marijuana pipe in his room got there without his knowing about it. He will not be honest about his chemical usage with you or anyone else—sometimes even his closest friends.

Tony sat across from me in the assessment and described his usage during the past three years. He had been drinking daily, cutting classes at school, and sometimes becoming angry and violent when drinking or using other chemicals. He would often pick fights with people he didn't know, especially when he was drunk. His friends would tell Tony to slow down and not drink so fast, but he didn't listen.

Tony began drinking before going to parties to "get in the mood." He recalled a situation when several of his friends told him that he was drinking too much and that he often got too "rowdy" when he drank. Tony's reply was one of surprise. He informed them that he didn't drink any more than any of his friends did. They couldn't argue with Tony. They were not aware of his extra drinks before the party.

Tony—age 15

The dependent alcoholic's self-deception does not end with dishonesty about his chemical-using behaviors; it carries over into lies about people, places, and things in order to present that "together" image he wants so badly to project. Covering up the amount of his chemical usage becomes a primary motivation.

"I can remember my mom confronting me when she suspected that I had been drinking. She sometimes would follow me up to my room at night when I came home and try to get close enough to me to smell my breath. She looked so dumb to me that I almost started laughing, but I didn't because I knew that she would get really mad. I guess I didn't realize then how sick I was getting or how much she worried about me when I came home after being out drinking at night. I guess I put her through a lot of worry. I'm just now beginning to realize that."

Olga—age 14

The dependent adolescent will try to convince others that he isn't drunk or stoned, no matter how much he has been drinking or using other drugs. His perception of himself stays the same as his disease progresses. He believes that he has everything under control, no matter how drunk or stoned he truly is.

Gary entered my office looking tired and worn out, apparently having difficulty focusing on me as he attempted to move toward the desk. He was obviously wanting to look like he had everything under control. Gary wasn't aware that it was obvious he was stoned.

He answered the questions in the assessment as accurately as he could, even if he was not completely honest about his usage. As we talked, he relaxed and began to look scared. He asked me about his daily nosebleeds and told me the amount of cocaine he was using daily. He described his blackouts while drinking and how he had nearly lost his girlfriend one night when he'd hit

*her while he was drunk. He continued to talk, and I lis-
tened.*

*Gary was admitted to the chemical dependency unit
that same day. He was scared and still trying to look
tough but seemed to be tired of his need to keep up a
façade for others. He seemed to be ready to make some
dramatic changes in his life.*

Gary—age 15

Dependent adolescents need the significant adults in
their lives to intervene and help them to seek help for
their addiction; left to their own devices, they will not
seek help for the real problem. Parents can be extremely
effective in providing the data necessary to admit the
dependent adolescent for treatment. Young chemically
involved adolescents will argue, fight, threaten to run
away, become isolated and withdrawn, or bargain for
another chance to prove that they can stay straight. The
odds are fairly high that their way will not work for any
length of time if they are dependent on chemicals. The
adolescent will go to any lengths to protect the thing
that has become most important in his life: his chemicals.

Treatment Considerations

Treatment is often needed for the adolescent with a
chemical addiction. Most adolescents who become addicted to alcohol and other drugs do not do so overnight, and it will take longer than that to correct the
problem. Recovery is a process that involves many levels of commitment, not only from the adolescent but
from his family as well.

Treatment for addictions is a relatively new field, be-

ginning in 1935 with the self-help group Alcoholics
Anonymous. Treatment for adolescents is an even
newer field, with the emergence of the first adolescent
inpatient chemical dependency treatment program in the
Minneapolis–St. Paul area of Minnesota. The types of
programs established there in the early 1970s became
known as the Minnesota model of treatment. In this
model, chemical dependency was termed a disease.

The disease model treats addiction to mood-altering
chemicals as primary, stating that harmful dependencies, left untreated, are progressive and fatal. This
model has reduced the stigma often related to chemical
addictions by encouraging addicted people to seek treatment for a disease. It is believed that millions of people
have received help and gone on to lead healthy, productive lives thanks to treatment and their subsequent
decision to remain abstinent and chemical free.

The Minnesota model of treatment uses a multidisci-
plinary treatment team approach, with a combination of
recovering and nonrecovering staff to address the many
aspects of the disease, from the emotional, physical, and
social ramifications to the spiritual and family concerns
of the patients. This approach to treatment offers education for both the patient and his family, the underlying
premise being that the patient should understand his disease better than anyone else and be fully accountable
for his own program of recovery.

In addition to education, the patient and his family
are involved in group, individual, and family counseling. Families who are adversely affected by living with
an alcoholic or drug addict can readily observe what the
addiction has done to their loved one but cannot as easily recognize the effect that addiction has had on them.
Families may suffer from the "isms" of alcoholism—
that is addictions to food, prescription drugs, gambling,

work, and so on. Although these other addictions may, at first glance, seem to be much less severe than the alcoholism or other drug addiction, they are often just as life-threatening.

Other family members will need to understand the behavior, known as codependency, which developed along with the addictive process in their child. Their love for their son or daughter encouraged them to protect and rescue the child, which only prolonged the disease process. The entire family, including the siblings of the adolescent patient, need treatment to recognize and deal with their issues of loss and grief. The family will need to begin its own healing process to address the impact that addiction has had on their lives.

Two types of programs are available to treat the disease of addictions in the adolescent population; the inpatient or residential model of treatment and the outpatient model. Many programs offer both components.

Inpatient Treatment Models

Inpatient programs are often highly recommended for adolescents. The adolescent who is removed from his immediate environment and drug-using friends while attempting to stay clean and sober generally has a much better chance of attaining abstinence. Second, many adolescents, due to their strong need for peer acceptance and support, benefit from living in a community of other adolescents who are also working to overcome alcohol and drug addictions. Moreover, in a structured environment the adolescent can more easily acquire the internal controls necessary to remain abstinent when it is time to return to his neighborhood, school, and family.

Inpatient treatment varies from state to state, but adolescents generally stay in inpatient treatment anywhere from several weeks to several months, often depending upon insurance benefits. The typical length of stay for most is twenty-one days, with others staying for only a couple of weeks. Inpatient programs also usually provide adolescents and their families with an aftercare program, often offered at no additional charge. Aftercare programs include education and group and family counseling components. Such programs are offered for as long as two years or more following inpatient care. Families and recovering patients are also encouraged to continue attendance at Twelve Step self-help groups, many of which may be offered at the treatment facility.

Inpatient program costs vary depending upon location; programs on the West Coast, for example, tend to be somewhat more expensive. Inpatient treatment charges also vary from one unit to another. If the program is located in a free-standing facility, it may be less expensive due to its lower overhead; hospital settings tend to charge higher daily rates (to cover additional charges for food, linens, biofeedback, and adjunct therapies such as physical and recreational therapy).

The alcohol and drug treatment field has become much more clinically accountable for providing quality outcome-based treatment services in the last several years. This has been due in part to the influence of insurance and managed-care protocols.

If an inpatient stay is approved by insurance or managed care, the length of stay is generally for a maximum of several weeks in order to stabilize the client, prior to referral to an outpatient setting. There is typically a capitated rate for inpatient stays, often ranging from five thousand dollars to ten thousand dollars.

The most critical component of any treatment program is its flexibility to meet the clinical needs of the patient, instead of the patient having to fit into an existing structure of the treatment program.

In communities where they are available, some adolescents will have the additional support of continuing their recovery care in an extended care facility, known also as a "halfway house." The majority of these facilities are located in the Minneapolis–St. Paul area of Minnesota, as well as in some other midwestern states such as Wisconsin and Iowa. Almost every state would benefit from such a program, however, as the toughest task for the newly sober adolescent is to return to the school environment, where the majority of drug using likely took place. For this reason, aftercare programming for the adolescent must be much more intensive than for the adult leaving treatment. Adolescent aftercare programs hold group, individual, and family therapy several times per week, in addition to the support of the Twelve Step self-help groups.

Outpatient Treatment Models

Outpatient programs, designed to treat chemical dependency while the client remains in his home environment, have become increasingly popular over the past several years. These programs, which allow the client to work on resolving problems while remaining in direct contact with school and home, are a positive alternative for adolescents who have a moderate to high degree of initiative to get clean and sober and who also have fairly strong family support.

Outpatient models of treatment for adolescents are generally highly recommended by insurers, as they afford many more subscribers treatment at much lower costs. Many insurance companies are now mandating that the adolescent attend an outpatient treatment setting initially, unless documented proof warrants an inpatient admission. This trend has become the norm in the past several years, as insurance companies struggle to keep down costs.

Outpatient treatment models have historically been designed for the adult client and include some very traditional outpatient counseling. A client will generally receive individual counseling once a week and then attend a self-help group such as Alcoholics Anonymous several other times during the week while staying clean and sober. This traditional treatment model does not work well with adolescents, who generally need much more intensive intervention. Ideally, the adolescent should receive several evenings of therapy from 4 to 9 P.M. during the week; sessions should include individual, group, and family counseling and Twelve Step support groups.

An effective program often runs for a minimum of six to eight weeks, with treatment intensity decreasing as the client moves toward acceptance of his chemical addiction and displays some level of comfort with sobriety and staying straight. Such a program often includes regular drug screenings to ensure that the adolescent is staying sober and may well require a commitment for involvement from all family members. Intensive outpatient programs may cost anywhere from three thousand to ten thousand dollars, depending upon the child's length of stay and the adjunct program components involved (e.g., biofeedback, recreational therapy, art therapy).

Adolescents are generally much more willing to try outpatient programs since in doing so they are able to maintain some degree of control over their lives. Their commitment to treatment allows them some continued freedom while working toward a life-style that no longer involves alcohol and drugs. Some adolescents manage to do fairly well in outpatient programs while remaining at home and at school. Others cannot withstand the pressure to say yes to drugs once they leave the treatment setting each day. Some states have established programs known as "day treatment." The adolescent returns home each night only to sleep, coming back each morning for treatment. The success rates of these programs tend to be higher, as they offer the adolescent a structured environment conducive to abstinence.

Many of these outpatient models for adolescents have not been in existence long enough to adequately measure their success. It seems fairly evident, however, that the adolescent who will succeed in this type of program must be motivated, have some family support, and not have a history of repeated failures at abstinence in an outpatient setting.

Economics of Treatment

As the treatment industry becomes more economically driven, there will continue to be an increase in outpatient programs for both adults and adolescents. There will also, most likely, be an increase in inpatient programs that respond to dual disorders, also known as "dual diagnosis programs." An adolescent with a dual diagnosis has both chemical addictions and psychiatric disorders. Dual disorders have become a focus of the chemical dependency field over the past several years, owing in part to the rising costs of health care and also to increased attention to other disorders, such as the depression often experienced by Children of Alcoholics who enter treatment for addictions. Many children from alcoholic families will display the signs and symptoms of codependency before ever taking a drink or using drugs, leading some researchers to believe that chemical dependency is a result of prior disorders.

New research also indicates that psychiatric disorders are significantly greater among those who become addicted to alcohol and other drugs, including greater susceptibility to depression, panic disorders, and phobic disorders. Yet this issue requires a great deal more research before any conclusive evidence may be reached that will present a clear picture of dual disorders.[1]

Many adolescents will present dual disorders in relation to their chemical addiction, including attention deficits, learning disabilities, adjustment reactions to adolescence, and depression due to sexual abuse or other responses to trauma. Many inpatient psychiatric programs for adolescent clients now have "substance abuse tracks" that treat the chemical addiction as well as the other disorders that are presenting problems in his life. Because of the dysfunctional characteristics of many families, some adolescents may use drugs "in context," meaning that their drug usage may be a response to other family trauma. Nevertheless, any continued chemical usage needs to be addressed.

An increased number of dual disorder programs have come into existence, driven by the economics of the treatment field. Insurance companies are moving toward a system of managed care that employs their own physicians and nurses to act as "gatekeepers," either granting or denying treatment stays based upon weekly case reviews. This new system is challenging treatment programs not only to improve their quality of care, but to create flexible programs that meet the standards of the insurance companies at lower costs.

Those who do not have the money for private treatment must rely on publicly funded treatment programs that offer treatment at either low cost or no charge.

These programs are primarily outpatient, although some states offer residential programs for alcohol and drug abusers. There is a vast need for these residential programs, however, and most have waiting lists of six months or more; clients are often "lost" in the system or incarcerated before they receive help.

With the increased focus on high-risk youth, more programs to treat alcohol and drug problems, teenage pregnancies, and gang-involved youth are springing up nationally. These programs often offer excellent services and provide support for youths attempting to make positive changes in their lives.

Evaluating a Treatment Program

The initial steps of evaluating a treatment program should take place in a chemical dependency assessment, either in an outpatient clinic at a school, with a psychiatrist or psychologist, or in an actual inpatient setting that offers assessments at no charge. The assessment, which will help to determine how serious the child's chemical addiction is and if inpatient treatment is warranted, should include conversations with both the parents and the adolescent so that the assessor receives a true picture of the case. As with the evaluation of any condition, it is always a good idea to get another opinion, especially if there are questions or concerns that were not adequately addressed in the first assessment. In addition, most assessors should provide the parents with at least three referrals to inpatient or outpatient treatment programs. Although the assessor may be able to answer many of the parent's questions, it is always a good idea to check the programs out firsthand so that fears and concerns can either be laid to rest or responded to by the facility staff.

Families who are beginning the process of shopping

for a quality treatment program will be overwhelmed by the number of programs and treatment modalities available. Many programs advertise their services on radio and television and in print. But most parents have no idea what constitutes a quality program as they begin their search.

Avoid programs that are reticent in answering your questions about their services or are not open to parent visits. One key characteristic of a quality program is openness to parents and referral sources, as well as a willingness to communicate its treatment philosophy. Parents may want to visit several programs to gain a feel for the program and the staff. Most first impressions are accurate and should be trusted.

Some basic criteria to look for in determining a quality adolescent program include the following:

1. The program should define addiction as the primary disease, even if clients have a dual diagnosis. Other symptoms can be treated, but if the addiction is not addressed, the adolescent will most likely relapse as soon as treatment is over.
2. The program should offer a combination of therapies, including education on the disease and its effects, and group, individual, and Twelve Step self-help groups geared to the adolescent client. Other components will vary but may include recreational therapy, biofeedback, art therapy, socialization skills, and/or assertiveness training. These are all geared specifically to the adolescent who has suffered developmental gaps and voids as a result of a chemical addiction.
3. Programs that mix adolescents and adult clients, particularly in a residential or inpatient setting, are generally less effective and should be evaluated fur-

ther. While having adults and adolescents attend lectures and Twelve Step groups together may offer some therapeutic benefits, housing them in the same facility is often disastrous. Adolescents need to be with adolescents and adults need to be with adults.

4. The program should provide a treatment team approach utilizing as treatment staff both recovering alcoholics and drug addicts and nonrecovering addicts. Staff who are recovering should be encouraged to work their own recovery programs by attendance at Twelve Step groups, just as patients are encouraged to make the Twelve Step groups a large part of their recovery program. Most programs believe that staff cannot ask clients to do what they themselves don't do. Since adolescents often "model" their behavior on that of the treatment team staff, this issue becomes even more critical.

5. In accordance with the disease model, adolescents should be taught about the serious chances for relapse and understand the tools they must employ to maintain sobriety once they leave inpatient or residential treatment.

6. The program should offer a holistic approach to treating the addiction, with emphasis on nutrition, healthy life-styles, and, in particular, a well-rounded fitness program. This type of program is especially crucial for an adolescent since young people often need to learn to channel their energies in a positive way to build self-esteem through an ongoing physical fitness program.

7. The program should have experience in treating addictions with adolescents, and the staff should be

comfortable discussing the rules and regulations with parents.

8. The program should have a high staff-to-patient ratio, necessary in an adolescent program not only to ensure adequate supervision, but to ensure quality treatment. In some large programs, (thirty beds or more) patients get lost in the shuffle and the adolescent may not receive adequate attention. Staff-to-patient ratios for adolescent programs should not exceed one staff member to every four patients. (If the ratio is one staff member to eight patients, for example, carefully investigate to determine whether the program offers a sufficient degree of individual assistance and supervision.)

9. The program should have a structured daily schedule, and weekend activities, including recreational programs that teach adolescents how to handle their leisure time now that they are sober.

10. The program should be accredited either by its state department of health or by JCAH (Joint Accreditation of Hospitals).

11. The program should be aware of the impact of growing up in an alcoholic family and should address this issue for the adolescent within the context of treatment while retaining focus on sobriety as the primary issue. Many adolescents drank and used drugs to mask the pain they felt in their family environments. Not addressing this issue can lead to relapse for the adolescent who will be returning home to a family member who may still be actively using alcohol and other drugs. Adolescents must learn to attain autonomy in their sobriety so that they can stay clean and sober no matter what the rest of their family is doing.

12. The program should offer a strong family compo-

nent that treats the *whole* family, including parents, younger siblings, and other relatives, as appropriate. This component cannot be stressed enough, as it is highly likely that the adolescent's younger brothers and sisters have been affected by the adolescent's chemical addiction, often "getting high" at very young ages. Programs that do not include a strong family component should be further evaluated for appropriateness, as they may decrease the chances for an adolescent to achieve and maintain sobriety for any period of time.

13. The location of the program should be convenient to the entire family, enabling participation in family treatment. Family involvement should be cost effective.

14. The program should offer a continuing care component, often known as aftercare, which allows patients and families to return for continued care up to two years after discharge from either inpatient or outpatient treatment.

The dependent adolescent becomes invested in learning the hard way as a result of his disease. Learning by one's mistakes is human, but the disease of chemical dependency only intensifies the pain of learning the hard way for the young person harmfully involved with chemicals.

There is an easier way. The attempts of both the young person and their parents or other significant adults to control the chemical usage problem has not been successful. The Twelve Steps of Alcoholics Anonymous offer a path to ending the pain. The basic promise of Alcoholics Anonymous, in its purest form, offers hope and inspiration for change and growth.

Some adolescents will achieve a great deal of their

sobriety within the rooms that house Alcoholics Anonymous. The only requirement for membership in AA is the desire to quit drinking. More alcoholics have been helped through this Twelve Step group than through any other treatment modality to date.

The initial premise that both the adolescent and his family are asked to contend with is the simple truth that they are powerless over alcohol and other mood-altering chemicals. At first, this entire concept is viewed as absurd. After all, the adolescent and his family have put considerable time and energy into trying to control, deny, and repress the problem. Giving up this control will be difficult, at best, and in most situations a frightening proposition. However, if one were to look more closely at the real situation, all that time, energy, and effort has produced no solid or long-lasting change, no matter how hard the family has tried to address the behavior caused by the chemical dependency.

The Twelve Steps of recovery provide the adolescent and his family with a spiritual base of understanding, strength, and hope that they have been unable to experience through their own efforts. Many families will turn to this simple way of living only when all else has failed and all other possibilities have been exhausted.

Step One: We admitted we were powerless over chemicals and that our lives had become unmanageable.

Step 1 of Alcoholics Anonymous offers the dependent adolescent a fresh look at his problem. He fully intended to use alcohol and other chemicals to have a good time, to be sociable, and to feel he is accepted by a group of peers. His experiences and his usage patterns are much different from those of his nondependent friends. The dependent adolescent does not know when to stop using chemicals. His usage had interfered with his daily functioning at home and at school, and he has to face serious consequences as a result of it. However, none of these consequences have been severe enough to deter him from using harmful chemicals.

The dependent adolescent becomes powerless over chemicals while the chemicals become more and more powerful in his life. The young person begins to use chemicals more frequently, and his life becomes more unmanageable. The unmanageability of his life appears in school, at home, and with his peer group.

Rick described the unmanageability in his life in many areas. He had been expelled from school because of excessive truancy and repeated suspensions. He was seventeen years old, and he had just completed ninth grade.

Rick had a sad and hurt look on his face as he continued with his First Step presentation. He had recently been involved with several friends who had participated in a murder, and it was obviously difficult for him to discuss it. Rick's friends had come to his house one evening very drunk and told him that they had just killed a man, a local alcoholic who lived on the streets. At first Rick didn't believe them and joked about the incident with them. Yet as they talked Rick realized that they were telling the truth. He was shocked but vowed that he wouldn't mention it to anyone.

The next morning Rick read about the murder in the paper. When he saw his friends the next day, he asked them why they had killed an innocent man. They told him that they had done it to see what it would be like to kill someone, like on television.

Rick became scared and called a local agency for alcohol and drug problems that same day. He stated that he wanted help for his alcoholism. He arranged a meeting with a counselor and went to the counseling session the next day. He was referred to treatment for second-stage alcoholism. The tragedy had been the impetus for Rick to seek help for a progressive disease that had already caused a great deal of pain in his life.

Rick—age 16

Fortunately most adolescents do not have to suffer the tragedy that Rick experienced through his friends to realize their dependency on chemicals. Admitting powerlessness over chemicals is essential for the young dependent adolescent; it is the step that allows him the freedom from his disease. Admitting powerlessness is the first step in experiencing freedom, in the purest sense of the word. Being honest with oneself and others is freeing for the dependent adolescent who has hidden behind his lies for so long. Taking an honest look at the unmanageability in his life helps the young person to see reality. Many young people were unaware of the danger in their lives while they were actively using chemicals.

The First Step in its truest form allows the young person to admit that he has not done a very good job at handling his chemical usage. To be able to say "I can't handle it. My Higher Power can. I believe I'll let Him" releases the young dependent adolescent from having to operate under the false impression that this disease can be controlled by will or by making intelligent decisions about his life. The disease is much more powerful in his life than he is. Accepting this simple truth is the most difficult aspect of the disease for most dependent adolescents.

Step Two: We came to believe that a power greater than ourselves could restore us to sanity.

Insanity can be described as behavior that is not rational. Any dependent person can behave in an insane way when under the influence of a mood-altering chemical. The dependent adolescent may go to apparently insane lengths to continue using his chemicals. Normal and healthy thinking becomes clouded as the young person loses all perspective on what is important in life, other than his relationship with his alcohol and drugs.

Dependent young people may do insane things while under the influence of chemicals; they may do equally insane things to ensure that they can obtain those chemicals. The insanity of the adolescent's thinking and behaving is illustrated by the following story of a young man who found himself in a dangerous situation while high one night.

Randy had been involved with alcohol and other chemicals since he was fourteen years old. He used alcohol, marijuana, and hallucinogenic drugs, primarily mescaline, on a regular basis. He described his insane behavior in group one day. He and his friends were drinking, and Randy decided to use the mescaline he had bought earlier that day. He blacked out and later could only recall bits and pieces of the evening. He did recall going to a party. The friend who was driving that night suggested that they all go buy more beer so they could continue partying. There wasn't room in the car for everyone, so Randy agreed to ride in the trunk of the car. He was really high by this time from the beer and the mescaline he had just taken.

Randy recalls being scared as he realized that his friend was driving recklessly and far too fast. He

*wanted out of the trunk and kept banging on the hood.
All he could hear was the roar of the engine just before
he passed out. By then he was too drunk to care.*

Randy—age 15

Randy was one of the lucky young people who suffered no serious consequences that evening. It was
frightening to listen to him describe the insanity of
some of his decisions while using chemicals. Now that
he had been sober for several weeks, recalling his insane behavior frightened Randy. He was beginning to
see the insanity of his behavior while using chemicals.

To continue to use chemicals despite harmful consequences is insane behavior. To continue with an "I can
handle my alcohol and other drugs" attitude is insane
behavior. To go to any lengths to obtain chemicals is insane behavior. The dependent adolescent will experience the insanity described in Step Two as his disease
progresses.

Step Two involves an honest appraisal of insane
thinking and behaviors. It also involves the identification of a power greater than oneself. Helping the adolescent to identify his own definition of a "power greater
than himself" is the core of Step Two.

Many adolescents have negative perceptions of God
or Higher Power. They have turned off to the concept of
organized religion, or to God. They may view their
Higher Power as a punishing force in their lives or as
something that hasn't come through for them when they
prayed for things to turn out the way that they wanted.
Reeducation on the concept of spirituality and working
through negative concepts of God may be necessary.

The importance of Step Two lies in having the young
person define his own Higher Power. This power
greater than himself may be the people in the Alcohol-

ics Anonymous meetings. Atheists have gotten sober using this simple definition. The important aspect of Step Two is accepting a power greater than they into their lives and giving up the chemicals (or false gods) that have been controlling their lives as their drug dependency has progressed.

Step Three: Made a decision to turn our lives and our will over to the care of God as we understand Him.

Having moved through Step Two, the young person is now asked to turn his life over to the care of his Higher Power. This is a frightening proposition for any drug-dependent person. It usually goes against every aspect of his nature. Controlling his drug addiction has not worked. He has still gotten drunk and high on chemicals and suffered painful consequences.

Step Three asks the dependent adolescent to believe that a power greater than himself can provide him with direction necessary to live a chemical-free life-style. It asks that he give up trying to manipulate and control the people, places, and things around him that he thinks will bring him happiness. It implies that he must give up his resentments of yesterday, the fears of tomorrow, and accept the way things are today. Step Three involves trust in a power greater than himself, a trust that everything will work out the way that it is meant to. Step Three asks the drug-dependent adolescent to practice acceptance in his life on a daily basis to stay sober and chemical free.

This simple step is a tough order for any recovering young person. He may decide that he will give some things up to the care of God but hang on to those things in which he has a deep emotional investment, such as a relationship or a desired goal. The peace and serenity that this step offers is considerable. Giving up control is like having a weight lifted off one's shoulders. For the drug-dependent adolescent, it's tough dealing with the reality that no matter how much he tries to manipulate and control the people and events in his life, things will work out the way they are going to work out.

John struggled with Step Three on a consistent basis. He had written out his Third Step work but kept putting off presenting this step to his counselor in the inpatient treatment unit. He could not see how he could possibly give up control of certain things in his life and trust that they would work out the way he wanted them to.

John and his counselor sat down to discuss the problems he was having in completing this step. The counselor suggested that John had a problem with self-will. Exploring how his self-will had not managed to keep John sober, John began to see the reality of this step. He explored how hanging on to his mistaken belief that he could manage and control the people, places, and things in his life could cause him to drink and use again. What if, after all of his best efforts, things did not work out the way he wanted them to? Then what?

John completed his step work and presented his Second and Third steps to his counselor. Following his step presentation, John had a new peaceful look on his face. He looked as though he had really taken a Third Step this time.

John—age 17

For adolescents in recovery, Step Three is closely related to the serenity prayer of Alcoholics Anonymous. "God, grant me the serenity to accept the things I cannot change, the courage to change the things I can, and the wisdom to know the difference." Recovering adolescents will hear this frequently throughout their treatment process, at their AA meetings, and through working a program of recovery on a daily basis.

Step Four: Made a searching and fearless moral inventory of ourselves.

The Fourth Step of Alcoholics Anonymous asks that the drug- and alcohol-dependent adolescent do the one thing he has been avoiding at all costs: take an honest look at himself. Dependent adolescents become accustomed to placing the blame on everything outside themselves as the source of all their difficulties. As long as they can focus on their anger and resentments toward others, they need not look at themselves or take responsibility for their own behavior and actions. They also do not have to create their own choices. When things go wrong, it is someone else's fault. They have not yet learned that, through their behavior, they are making choices every day.

Self-blame, guilt, and remorse are common to the recovering adolescent, especially for behaviors displayed while drunk or high or utilized to obtain chemicals. Dependent adolescents are usually much better at berating themselves than anyone else could ever hope to be. Feeling negative about themselves is familiar territory. Through their own negative thinking processes, they can turn a potentially positive situation into a negative one in a matter of minutes.

Fourth steps, although often painful, can produce very positive outcomes. The young person can be gently guided to see the importance of both the positives and the negatives in situations and, more important, in himself.

Who the adolescent really is has been buried underneath his chemical usage. Adolescents who become drug dependent have not had the necessary time to assess who they are. Their self-discovery process has been arrested. They have lost track of what is genuinely important. Some young people have not yet had the time to determine what is important to them, especially their values and goals. Their sense of self-confidence and self-worth have been damaged through their disease progression. They have become accustomed to fleeing from themselves to deny acknowledging the feelings, attitudes, and values they do have. In Step Four, they come face to face with themselves.

Jane, sixteen years old, was in an inpatient treatment setting for her chemical dependency for the first time. She had been using chemicals since she was thirteen years old and had a vague sense about herself. She began working on her Fourth Step and became aware of a key issue that had caused difficulties in most of her relationships.

Jane identified her false sense of pride as the source of most of her pain. Her false sense of pride created distance from the very people she wanted to be closest to emotionally. She was often lonely and afraid, but no one even knew it—she had worked hard to display just the opposite behaviors. She appeared aloof, distant, and "above" most of her peers. Her façade worked: people kept their distance.

Once Jane was able to be honest with others and with herself about her false pride, she was able to see that her behavior was self-defeating. Jane's Fourth Step inventory had been a turning point in her relationships with her peers and with her parents.

Jane—age 16

Many alcoholic and drug-dependent young people are quick to take other people's inventories and point out all the things they are doing wrong. If only *they* would change, then everything would be all right. The Fourth Step offers the young person the tools to begin a life-long process of wellness.

Step Five: Admitting to God, to ourselves, and to another human being the exact nature of our wrongs.

Step Five is sometimes referred to by young recovering adolescents as "dumping the garbage." It is an important step and involves trusting another human being enough to share the deep secrets of past chemical usage and the guilt, remorse, and self-blame that the young person is hanging on to despite his abstinence from chemicals.

Some adolescents are shocked to realize that an adult can sit and listen to their Fifth Step presentation with gentle caring and compassion. After all, how could anyone still possibly believe that they are an all-right person after hearing some of the worst things they have done?

Remember that the adolescent is going to be much harder on himself than anyone else is. The longer his secrets are kept inside, the more overwhelming and guilt-provoking they become. The dependent adolescent who hangs on to his past secrets also hangs on to the guilt and continues to "beat himself up" for events that took place in the past. How could people possibly love him if they really knew some of the terrible things that he did while using or to obtain his drugs?

Some dependent adolescents have stolen from their parents, from friends, or from stores and never gotten caught. They have used other people to meet their own needs. They have lied to people or damaged relationships they care very much about. Now sober, the young person in touch with his feelings and his own personal value system wonders how he could have done some of the "ugly" things he did to the people he cared about. What may be even more shocking for him is that these same people still care about him and love him despite his behavior.

Kim, fourteen years old, sat on the chair and leaned forward as she began her Fifth Step presentation. She felt guilty about so many things that she wasn't sure where to start. She seemed to feel the most guilty about an event that took place one night at her best friend's party. She had been drinking alone that day before going to the party. By the time she got to the party, she was already fairly drunk.

Kim had gone upstairs to the bathroom at her friend's house, and since no one was upstairs, she went into her friend's parents' bedroom. She opened the drawers, looking for money or jewelry that she could hock at a pawn shop. She couldn't believe that she saw a gold money clip with four fifty-dollar bills. As she stood there, she thought about all of the marijuana that even half that money could buy. She reached in and took two fifty-dollar bills, stuffed them into her jeans pocket, and went back downstairs to join the party.

The next day her friend called Kim at home—she had just gotten up, waking up late with a hangover—to say that she was grounded. Her parents were back from their out-of-town trip and had figured out that she had a party, and they'd also discovered that money was missing from their bedroom drawer. Kim listened, remembering the two fifty-dollar bills that were still in her jeans pocket. She didn't tell her best friend that she had taken the money. And she still has never told her that she took the money. In fact, she didn't hang around with her best friend anymore. They drifted apart after that.

Kim—age 14

Dependent adolescents completing their Fifth Step presentation need to understand that their behaviors while involved in an addictive disease were not always predictable nor indicative of the kind of person they are. They most need to hear "That's the way it was then. You did many things that you now regret. Your Higher Power is forgiving, and you now need to work on forgiving yourself."

Another human being has accepted them with all their flaws and negative behaviors. And they have not been judged on the basis of those behaviors. This is a revelation for newly recovering young people.

A complete and honest Fifth Step presentation can be evidenced in the nonverbal expression of many adolescents who complete this important step. Gratitude and relief often show on his face once an adolescent shares his most intimate hidden secrets and finds himself warmly accepted by another human being.

Rick had been worried all day about his Fifth Step presentation to his AA sponsor. He met with his counselor before his 1:00 P.M. step presentation to discuss his fear and anxieties. He trusted his sponsor but thought that his sponsor's opinion of him might change after he told him some of the things he needed to share. His counselor had assured Rick that this was another goal he needed to complete for himself.

Rick completed his Fifth Step presentation with his sponsor that afternoon. He and his sponsor came out of the counseling office as several of the staff, including Rick's counselor, were walking down the hall. With a big smile and a look of pride, Rick announced, "I did it!" There really was no appropriate response as I watched his counselor searching for the "right" words.

He simply walked over to Rick and gave him a big hug.
That's what working with young people is all about.

Rick—age 16

The Twelve Steps of Alcoholics Anonymous offer the recovering young person the basis for a solid sobriety and abstinence from chemicals. For most, merely quitting alcohol and chemicals is not enough. Approaching life from a different perspective is necessary for any recovering adolescent. Changing old patterns of thinking and solving problems helps the young person to achieve serenity and peace of mind, even in the midst of chaos.

The Alcoholics Anonymous program or other related programs such as Narcotics Anonymous offer the adolescent a group of sober and chemical-free peers that will be very important to his ongoing sobriety. The fellowship provided in these meetings offers the young recovering person healthy alternatives for socializing in a sober atmosphere and the support to continue his program of recovery.

Many adolescents recovering from alcoholism will lead healthy and productive lives as a result of utilizing a program such as Alcoholics Anonymous or Narcotics Anonymous. Such a program works if the young person is willing to commit to it, with the help of his family, peers, and, in many cases, a sponsor through the AA or NA program who has some experience in sobriety and can guide the adolescent through the "tough spots" of recovery. Young people who have learned this simple manner of living may not have to go through the years of pain that many of their adult counterparts experience in the progression of their disease.

CHAPTER 7

The Beginnings of Wellness:
The Family in Recovery

Families who become codependents in the addiction process of a son or daughter have many tools available to begin a process of recovery. For some, the process will begin while their son or daughter is still actively using chemicals. Others will not begin the recovery process until the son or daughter has entered a treatment program, whether it be inpatient or outpatient counseling. Families in recovery as codependents acquire a new perspective on the problem.

Prior to entering their own recovery program, parents may try to both handle and control the adolescent's chemical usage in a number of unsuccessful ways. They may have taken away privileges, hidden money or articles of value, screamed and cried, thrown away drugs and drug paraphernalia, denied the problem existed, withdrawn affection, or given the dependent adolescent special favors and attention. None of these attempts to control the problem have worked.

Families of chemically dependent adolescents experience a wide range of emotions as a result of living with an addicted young person. Parents involved in a codependency will repress their feelings in order to cope on a daily basis and to deny the pain they are experiencing from the addictive process. The most important discovery for codependents is that they have no control over alcohol and other chemicals. They are as powerless over mood-altering chemicals as is the dependent adolescent.

Most codependent family members have

- been preoccupied with their dependent adolescent's usage and found it increasingly difficult to concentrate at work and at home.
- made numerous unsuccessful attempts to control the adolescent's chemical usage.
- been affected either financially or legally by the adolescent's chemical dependency.
- experienced physical or emotional health problems caused by the traumatic events resulting from the dependency in the home.
- had negative consequences in their social life, marriage, or family life as a result of chemical dependency.
- harbored feelings of guilt and shame as the immediate relative of a chemically involved adolescent.

Acceptance of the disease, its consequences and effects, is necessary for recovery as a codependent. The dependency has become just as powerful for the codependent as for the addicted adolescent. The key lies in admitting powerlessness over the disease and the adolescent's chemical usage, a tough task for any parent. By admitting powerlessness, the parent or other significant adult must also make a decision to no longer enable the addicted adolescent. This means no more fixing things, no more going to any lengths to make sure the adolescent is not using alcohol and other drugs, no more battles with the addicted young person about his chemical usage. "Letting go with love" is a phrase heard often in treating the disease of dependency. The parent, teacher, or professional helper needs to realize that by enabling the adolescent he has perpetuated the vicious cycle of chemical dependency. The parent or other significant adult must begin to understand that each time he enables the adolescent, he is helping the young person to continue his usage without having to suffer any of the consequences brought about by his disease. Learning to let go and deal with the many feelings brought about by living with an addicted teenager are the beginnings of wellness for the family, the teacher, and the counselor, all of whom care about the young person and are invested in seeing him get help for his disease.

The Disease of Feelings for Families

Families may experience a wide range of emotions while living with an addicted adolescent. Guilt, anger, fear, hurt, and resentment are emotions that all codependents can identify with and relate to in discussing the disease progression in the person they love and care about.

Families need to acknowledge their feelings and discuss them in a supportive atmosphere that is safe and compassionate. They need to recognize that it is not normal for an adolescent living at home to refuse to follow any curfews, eat with the family, and communicate about where he is going at night. It is also abnormal to live from one crisis to the next with a sense of impending doom. Nondependent families do not live this way. Parents of children who do not have chemical addictions do not live this way. Parents of addicted adolescents do not have to continue to live this way.

Parents of chemically dependent adolescents can begin to explore how the disease progression has affected them. Chances are they have been so focused on their addicted son or daughter that they have been unaware of the effects of the progression of the disease. Most likely the changes have been very subtle, and they have lost touch with the many emotions that the disease has brought about in their lives.

The Disease Progression of Codependency[1]

Stage One: High Tolerance for Inappropriate Behavior In the beginning stages of codependency, the love that parents and other family members have for the adolescent motivates them to accept initial changes in behavior as part of adolescence; often they believe that their child is simply "going through a phase." The tolerance allows for acceptance of inappropriate behavior and a willingness to accept emotional pain, resulting in feelings of sadness, hurt, and embarrassment for the child and for themselves. In this stage, parents and family members will try harder to make the relationship work.

Stage Two: Denial of the Problem Eventually family members begin to make excuses, rationalize, and minimize the seriousness of the problem. They begin to use denial as a means of protecting themselves and, in the process, lose the ability to be honest with themselves. Although they may experience a wide range of emotions, including confusion, hurt, fear, and a great deal of internal conflict, they avoid talking about the problem and act as if nothing is wrong. Families will stay in various stages of denial throughout the disease progression of codependency.

Stage Three: Preoccupation At this stage family members, particularly parents, become preoccupied with the adolescent's behavior as his chemical addiction progresses. Parents will often move through a process of wanting to rid themselves of the problem entirely to wanting to control all of their child's actions and whereabouts. This swing from "I've had it" to "I'm taking over" results in feelings of anger, resentment, and hurt as parents struggle to understand the behavior that is causing so many problems. They become overly responsible, expecting less of their child and often lowering their standards for his behavior. Other siblings will usually be asked to "pick up the slack" and take over responsibility for chores around the house.

Stage Four: Energy or Love Shift At this stage in the codependency progression, the family may go through a shift in energies, particularly if parents have been policing their child's whereabouts. Parents will become very involved in activities away from home as a means of escape and may become highly susceptible to affairs with persons other than their marriage partner. The effects that chemical dependency has had on them can be observed in their withdrawal from the family. Their feelings of powerlessness and ineffectiveness as parents, and in other important areas of their life, make this shift in energy more understandable.

Stage 5: Tolerance Breaks At this stage of the disease, parents may be feeling a combination of rage and panic as they slowly watch their family changing and feel impotent to stop the process. Their guilt and shame at the inability to make any long-lasting changes in the family environment may cause them to overreact to problems. They may exhibit uncharacteristic emotional outbursts or emotionally abuse others. They are no longer able to deny the seriousness of the family problems but also do not know how to make changes.

Stage 6: Isolation Ultimately the parents will be discouraged and fearful, often dreading the next crisis that may arise as a result of their child's chemical addiction. They may move in and out of denial at this stage, at times knowing that there is a drug problem and at other times not wanting to believe it. Their withdrawal from family and friends will only increase their feelings of isolation. Many parents may have turned to tranquilizers or alcohol themselves at this stage, in an effort to handle the stress they are dealing with on a daily basis.

Codependency, like chemical dependency, is progressive and affects those who live with a person who is chemically addicted. The effects of the chemical dependency can best be seen in the many feelings and accompanying behaviors that parents and family members experience as they attempt to adjust to the disease.

Guilt
Many codependents, particularly parents, react to the knowledge of their child's chemical dependency with self-blame and guilt. Maybe they feel that they should have been less permissive, or seen the signs of dependency sooner, or listened to their child's cry for help when the problems in the home began. If only they had been more strict, if only they had been less strict, if only they hadn't moved to this neighborhood, if only

they hadn't worked so late at night, if only they had
been "better" parents. The "if only" list can go on and
on for parents and family members of the addicted adolescent.

*Shirley and Rob walked into my office with a defeated
look on their faces. They had been seeing counselors
for the past year in an attempt to handle Todd's behavioral problems. They stated that they had seen two psychiatrists in the past year at a local mental health
agency and had tried their best to address Todd's increasingly out-of-control behavior, with little effect.*

*Shirley and Rob were currently in marriage counsel-
ing because of their ongoing disagreements about how
to handle Todd, and both seemed to feel that their relationship had deteriorated during the past year.*

*Rob interrupted me to tell me about an event that
took place when Todd was approximately three years
old. He recalled becoming very angry with Todd and
spanking him much too hard for the behavior that he
was displaying. Rob was convinced that this was the
source of all of Todd's problems and still felt guilty
about the incident.*

*Todd was assessed for a chemical dependency prob-
lem that same day and was diagnosed in the crucial
phase of alcoholism and drug addiction. Although Shirley and Rob knew that Todd was involved in heavy
chemical usage, they were unaware of the disease progression and the accompanying behaviors present in the
addicted adolescent.*

*Shirley and Rob left my office in tears as their son
was being admitted to the chemical dependency unit.
They seemed both scared and apprehensive about
Todd's admission but at the same time they seemed relieved that he was going to be in a safe environment to*

receive treatment. These defeated parents left my office with some hope that Todd was going to get well.

Shirley and Rob
Parents

Parents of addicted adolescents need to understand that they are not responsible for their son's or daughter's addiction to chemicals. It does little good to dwell on the if onlys and the past mistakes that all parents make from time to time simply because they are human.

Anger

Living with an out-of-control adolescent who does not respond or listen to rules or parental expectations can trigger extreme anger and accompanying frightening feelings. Parents living with an addicted son or daughter may experience anger that they never knew they were capable of feeling, much less expressing.

Gary sat in the family session addressing his past hurts and resentments with his daughter Kim. He described his feelings of helplessness and rage when he became aware of Kim's drinking problem. Gary had been sober only a year when he noticed Kim's change in attitude and lack of caring toward family members at home. Kim was fourteen years old.

Kim had come home drunk one night, and Gary was shocked to see his fourteen-year-old daughter in that condition. When she walked into the living room and sat down, Gary remembers looking up at her. She was hostile toward him, smiling at him sarcastically when he asked her where she had been that evening. He tried to stay calm, but she became more hostile as they talked. Before he knew it, he was up and out of his chair, shak-

*ing Kim and throwing her down on the living-room car-
pet.*

*Kim got up, and Gary saw an obvious rug burn on
her face. She ran out of the room, and Gary began to
cry. He called his AA sponsor and arranged a meeting
for the next day. He also called the local alcoholism
clinic to inquire about placing a fourteen-year-old in
treatment.*

Gary
Parent

Anger and resentment can become powerful emotions
for families living day to day with a dependent young
person. Acknowledging the feelings can lessen their intensity and destructive expression. Anger expressed toward the drunk or stoned adolescent will only give him
more reason to drink and display uncontrollable behavior at home. Unaware of this, parents often find themselves reacting instead of responding to the behaviors of
the actively using adolescent.

Families of drug-dependent young people need to understand that their anger stems from their inability to
change the situation and their drug-dependent son or
daughter. Put in its proper perspective, anger becomes
less frightening and can be seen as a choice rather than
a reaction.

Hurt

Many families of drug-dependent adolescents operate
under the assumption that if their children only loved
and respected them more, they would change. Yet parents who look at the problem from this standpoint only
set themselves up for more hurt and more pain.

Although it is certainly natural to feel hurt and sad
about the adolescent's drug addiction and personality

changes, acting on those feelings by expecting the dependent adolescent to behave differently is unrealistic.

Hurt and sadness expressed to a drunk or stoned adolescent will have no lasting impact. Although the adolescent may promise that it won't happen again, the promise carries little weight. Parents need to understand that expressing their hurt and pain to their drug-dependent son or daughter is a start but certainly not the solution.

Babs could not stop crying as she described Joe's personality changes during the past year. He had become a different person. He was angry, resentful, and violent when he drank. Babs was scared when she was with Joe after he'd been drinking, and she found that she avoided him when he was home. She didn't even know her son anymore.

Babs seemed to hurt on a deep level. She continued to cry, stating that her father had died of alcoholism and that she could not stand to see her son go through this. I realized that I had just scratched the surface of Bab's pain.

Babs
Parent

Anguish resulting from an addiction in a family brings a deep sense of loneliness and failure to most parents, who frequently personalize their feelings and assume it is their fault that their son or daughter is chemically addicted.

An adolescent's chemical addiction is not a parent's fault; it is a disease that needs to be treated and arrested.

This concept can be especially difficult for the parent who is also the Adult Child of an Alcoholic. His or her

unresolved issues may make it very painful to acknowledge that a child has an addiction to chemicals. Since
most Adult Children of Alcoholics struggle with parenting issues in general, the out-of-control behavior often
exhibited by an adolescent with an addiction may over-
whelm them.

Many ACOAs struggle with a sense of worthlessness
and guilt, especially since they so want their child not
to feel as they did growing up. The losses they experienced as a result of living in a family with alcoholism
have often been so painful that they are absolutely committed not to hurt their children the way they were hurt.
As a result, many ACOA parents will accept the out-of-
control behavior of their child as normal for much
longer periods of time. This same pattern of parenting is
often seen in adoptive families who are very invested in
making the parent-child relationship a positive and ful-
filling one. These goals of parenting are positive and
well-meaning but may compel the family to experience
many crises and a great deal of hurt and pain before
help is sought to remedy their problems.

Fear

Many families of dependent adolescents experience
fear on a regular basis. Fear serves as a motivation for
many of the enabling behaviors that parents and other
family members display. Fear of what others will think,
fear of losing control of a son or daughter, fear of being
a "bad" parent, fear of an impending tragedy—all are
familiar feelings to families living with an addicted son
or daughter.

*Ken described his fear whenever his son, Keith, used
the family car at night and drank with his friends. Ken
was aware of Keith's drinking and often pleaded with*

him not to drink and drive. Periodically he would ground his son, but Keith would always promise that he had learned his lesson and would not drink while driving.

Ken would often lie in bed at night and pray that his son would not be involved in a serious car accident while drinking and driving. He would not fall asleep until he heard the car pull into the driveway. He lived in fear whenever his son used the car at night.

Ken
Parent

Fear of losing control of the child seems to be a painful reality for most parents of addicted teenagers. As their son or daughter becomes more and more out of control with their usage and accompanying behavior, most parents react with tighter controls and monitoring. Unfortunately, monitoring the adolescent's usage is a hopeless and futile task.

Don came into the assessment session well prepared. He had scheduled the session with me to determine if his daughter had a chemical health problem serious enough to warrant treatment. Don was an accountant by profession and had, in the midst of the confusion and chaos caused by his daughter's disease progression, kept his life organized and orderly.

As I began the assessment, I asked Don when he had first become concerned about Jenny's usage. He opened his briefcase and pulled out a file marked "Jenny 1982." He proceeded to describe to me each event, including time, date, and specifics of the situation when Jenny was drunk or stoned and displayed uncontrollable behavior. Each file contained significant events that

*Don had observed during the past months of living with
an addicted daughter.*

*I asked Don how he felt about the past year and a
half with Jenny, and he became solemn. Slowly and quietly he began to cry. He cried with relief, knowing that
the family was going to get some help and that Jenny
would receive treatment for her chemical addiction. He
never wanted to live this way again. He had seen what
the past year and a half had done to his daughter, but
he hadn't realized what it had done to him.*

Don
Parent

Family members become so focused on the chemical-
addicted son or daughter in the home that they are often
unaware of their feelings and their unhealthy styles of
coping with the chemical addiction. They, too, have
paid a price through worry, loss of sleep, loss of appetite, and, in some cases, ulcers and other physical health
problems.

Families need treatment just as much as the addicted
adolescent. It is particularly important for siblings of the
addicted adolescent to be treated, since most children
begin to use alcohol and drugs with their siblings or
peers. If one child in a family is addicted, it is highly
likely that the other children in the family have also ex-
perimented with drugs, often through the encouragement of an older sibling.

Primary prevention will need to take place with these
high-risk children who may move into an addiction of
their own. Their feelings also need to be explored, as
they may believe that their brother's or sister's chemical
abuse problem is their fault. They have most likely
learned to cover and lie for their sibling, often feeling
guilty about not being more honest with their parents.

They may have even been physically threatened by their addicted brother or sister and not been able to share their hurt and pain. All siblings, no matter what their age, have been affected in some way by a family member's addiction. They deserve the same education and information the parents receive so that they, too, can begin to make healthy choices in their life.

CHAPTER 8

Resources

Helpful Books

Another Chance: Hope and Health for the Alcoholic Family, by Sharon Wegscheider-Cruse (Palo Alto, CA: Science & Behavior Books, 1989). A description of the effects of alcoholism on the entire family.

Choicemaking, by Sharon Wegscheider-Cruse (Pompano Beach, FL: Health Communications, 1985). A description of codependency and how to begin making healthy personal choices in recovery.

Codependent No More, by Melody Beattie (San Francisco: Harper/Hazelden, 1987). A book describing, as its subtitle states, "How to Stop Controlling Others and Start Caring for Yourself."

A Guide for Adult Children of Alcoholics, by Herb Gravitz and Julie Bowden (Holmes Beach, FL: Learning Publications, 1985). Presented in a question-and-answer format that parents who are Adult Children of Alcoholics will find extremely helpful and informative.

It Will Never Happen to Me! by Claudia Black (Denver, CO: M. A. C., 1982). Especially helpful for Adult Children of Alcoholics in understanding the impact of the disease on them.

Keeping Secrets, by Suzanne Somers (New York: Warner Books, 1988). A personal account of growing up in an alcoholic family and the author's personal story of recovery.

My Dad Loves Me, My Dad Has a Disease, by Claudia Black (Denver: M. A. C., 1979). A workbook for young children growing up in alcoholic families.

My Name Is Davy, I'm an Alcoholic, by Anne Snyder (New York: Holt, Rinehart and Winston, 1977). A personal illustration of the progression of the disease from one young person.

A Parent's Survival Guide, How to Cope When Your Kid Is Using Drugs, by Harriet Hodgson (New York: Perennial Library, 1986). Identifies parental pitfalls to avoid when dealing with a child who has chemical dependency problems.

Raising Drug-Free Kids in a Drug-Filled World, by William Mack Perkins and Nancy McMurtrie-Perkins (New York: Harper & Row, 1986). Especially helpful for the parent who is interested in prevention with younger children.

Sarah T.—Portrait of a Teen-Age Alcoholic, by Robin S. Wagner (New York: Ballantine Books, 1973). An honest appraisal of the effects of the disease on young people.

A Time to Heal: The Road to Recovery for Adult Children of Alcoholics by Timmen Cermak (Los Angeles: J. P. Tarcher, 1988; New York distributor: St. Martin's Press). Provides a clear path toward the "Road to Recovery" for parents who were raised in alcoholic families.

Young Alcoholics, by Tom Alibrandi (Minneapolis: CompCare Publications, 1978). A no-nonsense view of adolescent alcoholism and addictions.

Young, Sober and Free, by Shelley Marshall (Center City, MN: Hazelden, 1978). Youth sharing their experience, strength, and hope of recovery by utilizing the Twelve Steps of Alcoholics Anonymous.

Self-Help Groups

Self-help groups have been around since approximately 1935, with the inception of Alcoholics Anonymous. Programs that are set up to allow members with similar problems to share experiences offer support within a nonjudgmental atmosphere. The fellowship created in Twelve Step groups is very powerful and by its structure encourages members to remain honest in order to stay sober and drug free. The spiritual aspects of the Twelve Steps form the core of the program, as members are offered a way of life that enables them to live "one day at a time." For adolescents, in particular, the love and caring they find in Twelve Step groups allows them to experience the love of others until they can begin to love themselves.

Today hundreds of Twelve Step self-help groups are based on the Twelve Steps of Alcoholics Anonymous (including Cocaine Anonymous, Narcotics Anonymous, Pot Smokers Anonymous, and the like); many of these groups have young people's meetings, which allow adolescents to form a network of sober peers to build new friendships and create a social circle of drug-free activities. All serve as an important aspect of recovery for the newly clean and sober adolescent.

For more information on Alcoholics Anonymous and other self-help groups, contact

Alcoholics Anonymous World Services
Box 459 Grand Central Station
New York, NY 10163

212-686-5454;

Cocaine Anonymous
6125 Washington Boulevard, Suite 202
Los Angeles, CA 90230

213-559-5833

Narcotics Anonymous
P.O. Box 9999
Van Nuys, CA 91409

818-780-3951

For additional information on young people's meetings:

International Conference of Young People in AA
Advisory Council
P. O. Box 19312, Eastgate Station
Indianapolis, IN 46219

Al-Anon, designed for families and friends of those emotionally involved with a chemically dependent person, is a self-supporting group of people who offer strength and hope and a new perspective for those concerned about a loved one's chemical usage. For more information on Al-Anon, contact

Al-Anon Family Group Headquarters, Inc.
P. O. Box 862
Midtown Station
New York, NY 10018-0862

212-302-7240

24-hour information line 800-356-9996

Families Anonymous groups were founded to provide
support to friends and relatives concerned about their
child's behavior problems, including those associated
with chemical dependency. These Twelve Step groups
are designed to provide members with support and a
new way to respond to the problem by changing their
attitude and focusing on what they can change. For
more information, contact

Families Anonymous, Inc.
P. O. Box 528
Van Nuys, CA 91408

818-989-7841

Codependents Anonymous groups (CODA) offer members a supportive environment to share their experiences, strength, and hope, whether they've been raised
in an alcoholic family or are dealing with an addicted
teenager. The only membership requirement for attendance at this Twelve Step–based meeting is the desire to
have healthy relationships. For additional information
on CODA, contact

Codependents Anonymous
P. O. Box 33577
Phoenix, AZ 85067-3577

602-944-0141

Tough Love groups address the growing concern of parents experiencing problems with a son or daughter using alcohol and other drugs. These groups offer a strong support to parents who must handle the chaos and trauma created by living with an addicted teenager.

Parents are taught the concept of "tough love"—a term heard often in the treatment of chemical-addicted adolescents. Initially parents may react with statements such as "Why, I could never be that cruel" or "My child would never forgive me if I did something like that." Simply put, Tough Love operates on the premise that given the deep denial of the disease, the softer, easier approach will not work with those involved in a fatal addiction. Creating consequences and letting the adolescent accept full responsibility for them is the quickest way to mobilize an adolescent to seek treatment.

Tough Love groups teach parents, with the support of other parents who have "been there," how to set clear and consistent expectations and to provide immediate consequences if their guidelines are not followed. This may mean that the adolescent will need to sit in jail overnight if arrested on a drunk-driving charge or that he may need to find another place to live if he refuses to follow the house guidelines. Although asking a child to move out is usually a last resort, it may be the incentive needed for the dependent adolescent to agree to enter treatment.

Tough Love groups seem to be especially helpful for parents who have younger children and thus a commitment to provide quality parenting to them, despite the presence of an affected adolescent. Parents provide each other with the necessary support to follow through on their plan and to receive feedback and continued guidance from parents who share the same problem. As with any self-help group, caution should be exercised if the parent does not feel comfortable with the approach recommended to them. In addition to these support groups, parents may want to seek counseling from someone trained specifically in chemical addictions or adolescent chemical addictions.

Tough Love groups are offered at no cost to the participants and are held in most cities throughout the United States. Tough Love handbooks and literature are available upon request from

Tough Love
P. O. Box 1069
Doylestown, PA 18901

215-348-7090
800-333-1069

Alateen meetings, designed for children who have relatives, including brothers, sisters, or parents, with addictions, offer a Twelve Step Program for young children. This simple program can provide the child with support, hope, and a safe place to discuss the problem with other children living with the same issue in their homes. At meetings the younger child can learn about alcoholism and other chemical dependencies. Some of their most important learning may be that their parent's or sibling's alcoholism or drug addiction is not their fault.

Having an opportunity to express feelings and discuss alcohol and drug problems created by family members serves as a healthy outlet for the child. Alateen meetings are highly recommended for Children of Alcoholic parents, who have a greater potential to develop alcoholism and drug dependencies.

The impact of a chemical addiction on a child cannot be underestimated. Many times the child has observed a

great deal more than parents admit to. He may have lied
and covered up for his older brother or sister on more
than one occasion, and he may have profound feelings
about what is happening in his family. As an important
part of the family, children deserve to be a part of the
process of getting well.

Alateen meetings use the same Twelve Step Program
of Alcoholics Anonymous and Al-Anon but gear their
material to the preteen and teenager living with a chemically addicted family member. The meetings allow the
child openly to discuss alternatives available to them
and provide them with various means of coping with
the problem. Alateen meetings are supported through
contributions and allow the child to remain anonymous
while seeking support and help. For additional information on Alateen, contact

Al-Anon Family Group Headquarters, Inc.
P. O. Box 862
Midtown Station
New York, NY 10018-0862

212-302-7240

Adult Children of Alcoholics groups

Within the last ten years increasing attention has been
focused on the effects of growing up in an alcoholic
home environment. One result has been the creation in
1983 of new groups known as Adult Children of Alcoholics (ACOA). ACOA groups offer support to any adult
who has grown up in a family with one or two alcoholic
parents. ACOA is also appropriate for adults who have
experienced various traumas (other addictive diseases
such as gambling, eating disorders, and the like) or
mental illness. Parents of adolescents with chemical ad-

dictions are also welcome, as ACOA will provide a safe place for them to come to terms with their past and provide them with new energy to focus on the present. For more information on Adult Children of Alcoholics groups, contact

Al-Anon Family Group Headquarters
or
Adult Children of Alcoholics
P. O. Box 3216
2522 W. Sepulveda Boulevard, Suite 22
Torrance, CA 90505

213-534-1815

Parent Information Groups

Some parent groups are available to educate parents on the effects of alcohol and other drugs on children. These groups really serve as clearinghouses that provide information in the form of literature and other educational tools.

Families in Action
National Drug Abuse Center
3845 North Druid Hills Road, Suite 300
Decatur, GA 30033
404-325-5799

National Federation of Parents for Drug Free Youth
1423 N. Jefferson
Springfield, MO 65802-1988

417-836-3709

Parents Resource Institute for Drug Education, Inc.
(PRIDE)
Hurt Building
50 Hurt Plaza, Suite 210
Atlanta, GA 30303

404-651-2548 or 800-241-7946

The National Council on Alcoholism was founded in 1944 by Marty Mann, the first woman to achieve sobriety through Alcoholics Anonymous. NCA has historically called attention to special groups such as adolescents and women, as well as the specialized issues of ethnic groups. NCA operates under the basic premise that alcoholism and other chemical addictions are preventable, treatable diseases. NCA can assist with finding quality inpatient and outpatient treatment programs in your area and provide education and information in the form of local self-help groups, literature, films, and prevention groups. Many chapters of NCA sponsor parent education and support groups. For more information, contact

National Council on Alcoholism
12 West 21st Street
New York, NY 10010

800-NCA-CALL (800-622-2255)

Children of Alcoholics Resources

The National Association for Children of Alcoholics was founded in 1983 to support Children of Alcoholics regardless of age by providing public and professional awareness through information and referral, to advocate

policies and protect the rights of Children of Alcoholics
to live in a safe and healthy environment, and to offer
professional guidelines for those who work with COAs.
Their elementary school program entitled "It's Elementary" (chapter 4), along with additional information, can
be obtained through

NACOA
11426 Rockville Pike
#301
Rockville, MD 20852
301-468-0985

BABES, a prevention program designed to teach general
coping skills to the young child, is now also available for
children up to eighteen years old and for the preschool
child from one and a half to three years old. BABES
(Beginning Alcohol and Addictions Basic Education
Studies) was founded in 1979 and by 1988 was reaching
more than a million children in forty states. The BABES
approach to prevention utilizes puppets and stories designed to teach decision-making, ways to handle peer
pressure, and ways to cope in a family where alcoholism
is present. BABES is a division of the National Council
on Alcoholism and can be contacted by writing

BABES, NCA-OD/*GDA*
17330 Northland Park Court
Southfield, MI 48075

800-54-BABES or 313-443-1676

Additional Resources

Students Against Drunk Driving (SADD) was founded in
1981, with chapters now found on most high-school

campuses across the United States. SADD offers education and prevention materials to students, parents, and educators. One of the most popular items is their "contract for life," in which students pledge to contact parents for transportation if they have been drinking. This contract is meant to prevent the young person from riding or driving following a drinking episode. For further information, contact

SADD
P. O. Box 800
Marlboro, MA 01752

617-481-3568

Mothers Against Drunk Driving (MADD) was founded in 1980 by a mother whose daughter was killed by a drunk driver. MADD provides education and prevention, with many local chapters offering victim assistance, advocacy, information, and referrals. Recently MADD gained national attention and increased awareness of the incidence of drunk driving by lobbying for tougher drunk-driving laws.

MADD
669 Airport Freeway, Suite 310
Hurst, Texas 76053

817-268-6233

Friday Night Live, a group run by students with an adult faculty adviser, organizes and offers chemical-free activities to students. Especially popular in California, these groups teach adolescents how to have fun while sober, with both recovering and nonrecovering students in attendance at FNL events.

Friday Night Live
California Department of Alcohol and Drug Programs
11 Capitol Mall, Room 223
Sacramento, CA 95814

916-445-7456

CHAPTER 9

Healthy Perspectives

Chemically dependent adolescents are receiving treatment for their addiction and remaining sober today thanks to increased knowledge about adolescent addictions and the growing number of facilities available in the treatment of this disease. Families as well are actively involved in a recovery process through their attendance at self-help groups and their acceptance of a son or daughter's addiction to mood-altering chemicals. Entire families are being afforded the opportunity to rebuild the family unit through the growth that a dependency in the family has offered them.

Families in recovery express their gratitude in Al-Anon, Tough Love, Families Anonymous, and Alcoholics Anonymous meetings throughout the country. None of these families will say that the process has been easy. None will tell you that being the parent of an addicted teenager is simple or painless. They will tell you that they have grown and learned about the disease and themselves. They will most likely also tell you that their families have come a long way toward addressing problems and providing the support necessary to function as a family unit, despite the problems they may have to face in the days ahead.

It has been my experience that families and family members do not change and grow as human beings unless they are in such emotional pain that they have little choice in the matter. It is human nature to throw up defenses, and to deny, to avoid facing a problem until we feel that we have no choice but to change. Sometimes that change may mean the acceptance of a problem that would be much easier to avoid. Or it may mean that all our own resources have been exhausted, and outside help is needed to address the problem. This very act of surrender, of "letting go," has led many families into a recovery process and the peace of mind and serenity that recovery offers.

A greater number of families and adolescents are recovering from chemical addictions and leading healthy and spiritual lives. Adolescents are now entering treatment much earlier in their disease progression, increasing their chances for a lasting recovery. Self-help groups such as Young People's Alcoholics Anonymous are springing up across the country, and their meetings continue to be well attended. Many states throughout the country are at last offering a growing number of inpatient units designed to treat the alcoholic and addicted adolescent. Most likely, the specialized field of adolescent chemical dependency will continue to grow, as it has some catching up to do with the current services available to adult alcoholics and addicts.

Nationally, task forces and concerned legislators are meeting to research and propose programming to treat the problem of adolescent drug addiction. The topic continues to be of major interest for state agencies throughout the United States. The positive energy created by focusing on the problem has brought about changes that have significantly affected the number and quality of services now available in the treatment of adolescent chemical addictions.

A new movement is slowly taking hold on both high school and college campuses across the United States: sobriety! Nonalcoholic activities, including dances, graduation parties, proms, and after-game parties, are increasing. Friday Night Live chapters—which organize alcohol- and drug-free activities in communities—are becoming popular.

Campaigns geared to address the high incidence of drinking-driving accidents among young people have gathered momentum, with chapters of SADD and MADD springing up on high-school and college campuses nationally. A recent report indicates that SADD has already received over four hundred thousand requests for its parent-student contract. Over the past decade, MADD has gathered 2.8 million members to aid in their advocacy and educational endeavors. Currently, nearly 80 percent of all high schools in the United States have SADD chapters and four hundred communities have MADD chapters.[1]

Even more important, recent statistics cited by SADD indicate that alcohol-related automobile deaths among fifteen- to nineteen-year-olds plunged to 2,170 in 1988 from a peak of 6,281 in 1982. Health awareness has accounted for some of the changes, with a new emphasis on being clean and sober as the "vogue" thing to do.

Some efforts are beginning to pay off as communities pull together to fight the war on drugs. However, we cannot become complacent. We are only beginning to see some of the results of the hard work that has been going on for the past ten years. We have new problems—problems with gangs, with new designer drugs like "ice," with teenagers using drugs, including alcohol, at even younger ages. No single government policy or program can be expected to win the war on drugs. Community efforts are needed. Education is needed. Prevention programs are needed. And for some of these answers, we need to look to the kids who have already been there.

Healthier life-styles are being introduced to young people today, and recovery from a progressive disease is no longer something to be ashamed of. As more adolescents become sober, they are returning to their schools as "ambassadors," doing the footwork to educate peers, parents, and teachers on teenage alcoholism and drug addiction.

Adolescents with chemical addictions have become both the student and the teacher of the disease. They have learned that alcoholism and drug addiction can happen quickly and that arresting the disease is only the first step toward recovery. They have learned new steps toward freedom from an addiction and have gotten to know themselves better in the process. And they have made some very adult decisions about the quality of their lives chosen through recovery.

They have been our teachers as well. They have taught us that for those with an addiction to alcohol and other chemicals, life can be short. They have taught us that they are tomorrow's children and deserve to live healthy and happy lives. And they have taught us that living with alcoholism can be a blessing and a chance for rebirth in recovery. Their gratitude to those who have loved them until they could begin to love themselves can best be described by Curt, a sixteen-year-old in treatment for his chemical addiction.

You were with me for a while
You gave me something I never knew was mine
An awareness of what I think and feel
Most of all you taught me to be real

A true man isn't afraid to cry
Up to now I thought it was a lie
As I look back though, I see
The most important gift I got from you was me

You mean more to me than you know
You taught me how to risk and grow
And as I look back now, I see
You're the one who gave me back me.

Curt—age 16

Chapter 1

1. "Alcoholism Is Linked to a Gene." *The Wall Street Journal*, April 18, 1990. The article, written by staff reporter Sonia L. Nazario, for *The Wall Street Journal*, also refers to the Swedish study.
2. Ibid.
3. Risk factors for adolescents who may develop chemical addictions are based on the work of Dr. J. David Hawkins and Dr. Richard F. Atalanc, San Diego, California; as part of their research into the causes of alcoholism.
4. From the findings of the National Association for Children of Alcoholics, based in Rockville, Maryland.
5. Information on Native Americans from Kathy Brown Ramsperger, "Salvation for an Invisible People," *The Counselor*, May/June 1989, pp. 21–23.
6. Information on Hispanics and chemical dependency from "Treatment and Recovery Issues for the Addicted Hispanic," *The Counselor*, May/June 1989, pp. 29–30.
7. Cheryl Davenport-Dozier, "The African American and Alcoholism," *The Counselor*, May/June 1989, pp. 34–35. Also, information on Alcoholism in the African American community from Barbara Yoder, *The Recovery Resource Guide*. New York: Simon and Schuster, 1990, pp. 74–75.
8. Statistics from George Marcelle, "Kids Under the Influence Report," 1989 National Council on Alcoholism; available from Films for the Humanities, 743 Alexander Rd., Princeton, NJ 08540. Statistics also from the National Council on Alcoholism

Fact Sheet on Alcohol and Youth, 1989, 12 West 21st St., New York, NY 10010.

9. Statistics from Marcelle, op. cit., and from Yoder, op. cit., pp. 184–215.

Chapter 2

1.–8. Information on drugs from Barbara Yoder, *Recovery Resource Guide*, chapters on Street Drugs, Cocaine, and Marijuana, New York: Simon and Schuster, 1990, pp. 184–215; and The Michigan Clearinghouse for Substance Abuse Information, East Lansing, MI 48823.

9. Statistics from the National Council on Alcoholism Fact Sheet, 1989, 12 West 21st St., New York, NY 10010.

Chapter 3

1. Erik Erickson, *Identity and Youth in Crisis*, New York, W. W. Norton, 1968.

2. From the National Council on Alcoholism Fact Sheets on Fetal Alcohol Syndrome, March 1989, 12 West 21st St., New York, NY 10010.

Chapter 4

1. From the Charter Statement of the National Association for Children of Alcoholics, in Rockville, Maryland.

Chapter 5

1. David & Phyllis York; *Toughlove*. New York, Bantam, 1980.

Chapter 6

1.   Information on dual diagnosis from Barbara Yoder, *Recovery Resource Guide,* New York: Simon and Schuster, 1990, pp. 270–271.

Chapter 7

1.   Codependency progression taken in part from works by John Friel and Robert Subby in "Codependency: An Emerging Issue," Health Communications, Inc., Pompano Beach, FL., pp. 34–44.

Chapter 9

1.   Information from "Youthful Sobriety Tests Liquor Firms," by Marj Charlier, *Detroit Free Press*, June 15, 1990.